ACCA EXAMINATION KIT

Part 1

Paper 1.1

Preparing Financial Statements (United Kingdom Stream)

ISBN 1 84390 145 5

Second Edition

British Library Cataloguing-in-Publication data

A catalogue record for this book is available from the British Library.

We are grateful to the Association of Chartered Certified Accountants for permission to reproduce past examination questions. The solutions have been prepared by The Financial Training Company.

Published by

The Financial Training Company
22J Wincombe Business Park
Shaftesbury
Dorset
SP7 9QJ

Contents

Pilot paper

Syllabus

Paper 1.1 Preparing Financial Statements (UK)

Aim

To develop knowledge and understanding of the techniques used to prepare year-end financial statements, including necessary underlying records, and the interpretation of financial statements for incorporated enterprises, partnerships and sole traders.

Objectives

On completion of this paper candidates should be able to:

- describe the role and function of external financial reports and identify their users
- explain the accounting concepts and conventions present in generally accepted accounting principles
- record and summarise accounting data
- maintain records relating to fixed asset acquisition and disposal
- prepare basic financial statements for sole traders, partnerships, incorporated enterprises and simple groups
- appraise financial performance and the position of an organisation through the calculation and review of basic ratios
- demonstrate the skills expected in Part 1.

Position of the paper in the overall syllabus

No prior knowledge is required before commencing study for Paper 1.1. There is some connection with Paper 1.2 Financial Information for Management in the areas of performance management and data recording. There are no links with Paper 1.3 Managing People.

The basic financial accounting in Paper 1.1 is developed in Paper 2.5 Financial Reporting and Paper 3.6 Advanced Corporate Reporting. Knowledge from Paper 1.1 provides the background to Paper 2.6 Audit and Internal Review.

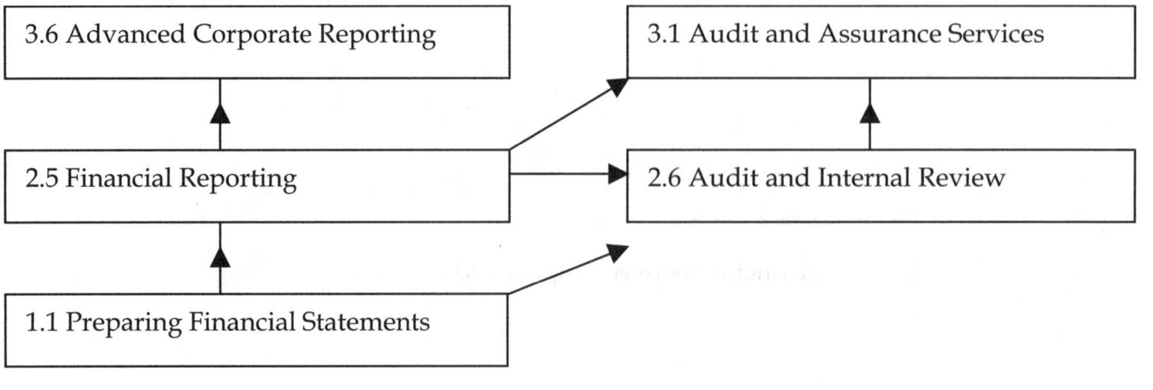

Syllabus content

1 General framework

(a) Types of business entity - limited companies, partnerships and sole traders.

(b) Forms of capital and capital structures in limited companies.

(c) The role of the Financial Reporting Council, the Financial Reporting Review Panel, Accounting Standards Board (ASB) and the Urgent Issues Task Force.

(d) Application of Financial Reporting Standards (FRSs) and Statements of Standard Accounting Practice (SSAPs) to the preparation and presentation of financial statements.

(e) The ASB's Statement of Principles for Financial Reporting (Chapters 1, 2 and 3 only).

2 Accounting concepts and principles

(a) Basic accounting concepts and principles as stated in the ASB's Statement of Principles for Financial Reporting.

(b) Other accounting concepts

(i) historical cost
(ii) money measurement
(iii) entity
(iv) dual aspect
(v) time interval.

3 Double-entry bookkeeping and accounting systems

(a) Double-entry bookkeeping and accounting systems

(i) form and content of accounting records (manual and computerised)
(ii) books of original entry, including journals
(iii) sales and purchase ledgers
(iv) cash book
(v) general ledger
(vi) trial balance
(vii) accruals, prepayments and adjustments
(viii) asset registers
(ix) petty cash

(b) Confirming and correcting mechanisms

(i) control accounts
(ii) bank reconciliations
(iii) suspense accounts and the correction of errors.

(c) General principles of the operation of a value added tax.

(d) Computerised accounting systems

4 Accounting treatments

(a) Fixed assets, tangible and intangible

(i) distinction between capital and revenue expenditure

(ii) accounting for acquisitions and disposals

(iii) depreciation - definition, reasons for and methods, including straight line, reducing balance and sum of digits

(iv) research and development

(v) elementary treatment of goodwill.

(b) Current assets

(i) stock (excluding long-term contracts)
(ii) debtors, including accounting for bad and doubtful debts
(iii) cash.

(c) Current liabilities and accruals.

(d) Shareholders' equity.

(e) Post balance sheet events.

(f) Contingencies.

5 **Financial statements**

(a) Objectives of financial statements.

(b) Users and their information needs.

(c) Key features of financial statements

(i) balance sheet

(ii) profit and loss account

(iii) cash flow statement

(iv) notes to the financial statements (examined to a limited extent – see (d) (iii) below).

(d) Preparation of financial statements for:

(i) sole traders, including incomplete records techniques.

(ii) partnerships

(iii) limited companies, including profit and loss accounts and balance sheets for internal purposes and for external purposes in accordance with Companies Act 1985 formats and preparation of basic cash flow statements for limited liability companies (excluding group cash flow statements). The following notes to the financial statements will be examinable and no others:

- Statement of movements in reserves
- Fixed assets
- Exceptional and extraordinary items
- Post balance sheet events
- Contingent liabilities and contingent assets
- Research and development expenditure

(iv) groups of companies - preparation of a basic consolidated balance sheet for a company with one subsidiary.

6 **Interpretation**

(a) Ratio analysis of accounting information and basic interpretation.

Excluded topics

The syllabus content outlines the area for assessment. No questions will be asked on: clubs and societies, partnerships other than the preparation of financial statements for partnerships.

Key areas of the syllabus

The objective of Paper 1.1, Preparing Financial Statements, is to ensure that candidates have the necessary basic accounting knowledge and skill to progress to the more advanced work of Paper 2.5 Financial Reporting. The two main skills required are:

- the ability to prepare basic financial statements and the underlying accounting records on which they are based
- an understanding of the principles on which accounting is based.

The key topic areas are as follows:

- preparation of financial statements for limited companies for internal purposes or for publication
- preparation of financial statements for partnerships and sole traders (including incomplete records)
- basic group accounts - consolidated balance sheet for a company with one subsidiary
- basic bookkeeping and accounting procedures
- accounting conventions and concepts
- interpretation of financial statements
- cash flow statements
- accounting standards – SSAPs 9, 13 and 17 plus FRSs 1, 3, 18 and the relevant sections of FRSs 12 and 15.

Approach to examining the syllabus

The examination is a three hour paper constructed in two sections. Both sections will draw from all parts of the syllabus and will contain both computational and discursive elements.

		Number of Marks
Section A:	25 compulsory multiple choice questions (2 marks each)	50
Section B:	5 compulsory short form questions (10 marks each)	50
		100

Additional information

Candidates need to be aware that questions involving knowledge of new examinable regulations will not be set until at least six months after the last day of the month in which the regulation was issued.

The Study Guide provides more detailed guidance on the syllabus. Examinable documents are listed in the 'Exam Notes' section of the *Students' Newsletter*.

Approach to objective test questions

The objective test questions will comprise a question with four possible answers. For example,

1 What is the world's tallest mountain?

- **A** Ben Nevis
- **B** K2
- **C** Mount Everest
- **D** Mount Snowdon

You have to select the correct answer (which in the above example is of course **C**).

In the examination, however, the incorrect answers, called distractors, may be quite plausible and are sometimes designed if not exactly to mislead you, to nevertheless be the result of fairly common mistakes.

The following is a suggested technique for answering these questions, but as you practise for the examination you have to work out a method which suits you.

Step 1
Read all the questions, but not necessarily the answers. Select the ones which you think are the most straightforward and do them first.

Step 2
For more awkward questions, some people prefer to work the question without reference to the answers which increases your confidence if your answer then matches one of the options. However some people prefer to view the question with the four answers as this may assist them in formulating their answer.

This is a matter of personal preference and you should perhaps practise each to see which you find most effective.

Step 3
If your answer does not match one of the options you must:

(a) Re-read the question carefully to make sure you have not missed some important point.

(b) Re-work your solution eliminating any mistakes.

(c) Beware of the plausible distractors but do not become paranoid. The examiner is not trying to trip you up and the answer should be a straightforward calculation from the question.

Step 4
Time allocation. As with all questions you must not overrun your time. The questions are technically worth only two marks each which is about three to four minutes per question. It is very easy to get bogged down. If you cannot get one of the right answers then move on to the next question.

Step 5
When you have finished all the questions go back to the ones you have not answered.

Keep an eye on the clock – don't overrun the time allocation.

If you really cannot do it, **have a guess**. You are not penalised for wrong answers. **Never leave any questions unanswered.**

Multiple choice questions

1 If the owner of a business takes goods from stock for his own personal use, the accounting concept to be considered is the:

A prudence concept

B capitalisation concept

C money measurement concept

D separate entity concept

---

2 A business has opening stock of £12,000 and closing stock of £18,000. Purchase returns were £5,000. The cost of goods sold was £111,000.

Purchases were:

A £100,000

B £110,000

C £116,000

D £122,000

---

3 A business had a balance at the bank of £2,500 at the start of the month. During the following month, it paid for materials invoiced at £1,000 less trade discount of 20% and cash discount of 10%. It received a cheque from a debtor in respect of an invoice for £200, subject to cash discount of 5%.

The balance at the bank at the end of the month was:

A £1,970

B £1,980

C £1,990

D £2,000

---

4 An error of commission is one where:

A a transaction has not been recorded

B one side of a transaction has been recorded in the wrong account, and that account is of a different class to the correct account

C one side of a transaction has been recorded in the wrong account, and that account is of the same class as the correct account

D a transaction has been recorded using the wrong amount

---

5 Goodwill is most appropriate classed as:

A a fixed asset

B an intangible asset

C a fictitious liability

D a semi-fixed asset

---

6 The double-entry system of bookkeeping normally results in which of the following balances on the ledger accounts?

	Debit balances	*Credit balances*
A	Assets and revenues	Liabilities, capital and expenses
B	Revenues, capital and liabilities	Assets and expenses
C	Assets and expenses	Liabilities, capital and revenues
D	Assets, expenses and capital	Liabilities and revenues

---

7 A business commenced with capital in cash of £1,000. Stock costing £800 is purchased on credit, and half is sold for £1,000 plus VAT, the customer paying in cash at once.

The accounting equation after these transactions would show:

A assets £1,775 less liabilities £175 equals capital £1,600

B assets £2,175 less liabilities £975 equals capital £1,200

C assets £2,575 less liabilities £800 equals capital £1,775

D assets £2,575 less liabilities £975 equals capital £1,600

---

8 A sole trader had opening capital of £10,000 and closing capital of £4,500. During the period, the owner introduced capital of £4,000 and withdrew £8,000 for her own use.

Her profit or loss during the period was:

A £9,500 loss

B £1,500 loss

C £7,500 profit

D £17,500 profit

---

9 A business has made a profit of £8,000 but its bank balance has fallen by £5,000. This could be due to:

A depreciation of £3,000 and an increase in stocks of £10,000

B depreciation of £6,000 and the repayment of a loan of £7,000

C depreciation of £12,000 and the purchase of new fixed assets for £25,000

D the disposal of a fixed asset for £13,000 less than its book value

---

10 A business operates on a gross profit margin of $33\frac{1}{3}$%. Gross profit on a sale was £800 and expenses were £680.

The net profit percentage is:

A 3.75%

B 5%

C 11.25%

D 22.67%

---

11 A company has authorised share capital of 50,000 5% preference shares of £2 each and 500,000 ordinary shares with a par value of 20p each. All of the preference shares have been issued, and 400,000 ordinary shares have been issued at a premium of 30p each. Interim dividends of 5p per ordinary share plus half the preference dividend have been paid during the current year. A final dividend of 15p per ordinary share is declared.

The total of dividends payable for the year is:

A £82,500

B £85,000

C £102,500

D £105,000

---

12 A fixed asset costing £12,500 was sold at a book loss of £4,500. Depreciation had been provided using the reducing balance, at 20% per annum since its purchase.

Which of the following correctly describes the sale proceeds and length of time for which the asset had been owned?

	Sale proceeds	*Length of ownership*
A	Cannot be calculated	Cannot be calculated
B	Cannot be calculated	2 years
C	£8,000	Cannot be calculated
D	£8,000	2 years

---

13 Your company auditor insists that it is necessary to record items of plant separately and to depreciate them over several years but that items of office equipment, such as hand-held stapling machines, can be grouped together and written off against profits immediately.

The main reason for this difference in treatment between the two items is because:

A treatment of the two items must be consistent with treatment in previous periods

B items of plant last for several years, whereas hand-held stapling machines last only for months

C hand-held stapling machines are not regarded as material items

D items of plant are revalued from time to time, whereas hand-held stapling machines are recorded at historical cost

---

14 On 1 July 1997, your fixed asset register showed a net book value of £47,500. The ledger accounts showed fixed assets at cost of £60,000 and provision for depreciation of £15,000. It was discovered that the disposal of an asset for £4,000, giving rise to a loss on disposal of £1,500, had not been recorded in the fixed asset register.

After correcting this omission, the fixed asset register would show a balance which was:

A £3,000 lower than the ledger accounts

B £1,500 lower than the ledger accounts

C equal to the ledger accounts

D £1,000 higher than the ledger accounts

---

15 The bank statement at 31 October 1997 showed an overdraft of £800. On reconciling the bank statement, it was discovered that a cheque drawn by your company for £80 had not been presented for payment, and that a cheque for £130 from a customer had been dishonoured on 30 October 1997, but that this had not yet been notified to you by the bank.

The correct bank balance to be shown in the balance sheet at 31 October 1997 is:

A £1,010 overdrawn

B £880 overdrawn

C £750 overdrawn

D £720 overdrawn

---

16 A credit entry of £450 on X's account in the books of Y could have arisen by:

A X buying goods on credit from Y

B Y paying X £450

C Y returning goods to X

D X returning goods to Y

---

17 The *main* purpose of an audit is to:

A detect errors and fraud

B ensure that the accounts are accurate

C determine whether the accounts show a true and fair view of the financial state of the organisation

D ensure that all transactions have been recorded in the books of account

---

18 A computerised spreadsheet package is *most* suitable for:

A recording the dual effect of accounting transactions

B maintaining an audit trail of transactions

C performing bank reconciliations

D preparing a cash budget

---

19 Where a transaction is entered into the correct ledger accounts, but the wrong amount is used, the error is known as an error of:

A omission

B original entry

C commission

D principle

---

20 At 1 September, the motor expenses account showed four months' insurance prepaid of £80 and petrol accrued of £95. During September, the outstanding petrol bill is paid, plus further bills of £245. At 30 September there is a further outstanding petrol bill of £120.

The amount to be shown in the profit and loss account for motor expenses for September is:

A £385

B £415

C £445

D £460

---

21 Your organisation sold goods to PQ Limited for £800 less trade discount of 20% and cash discount of 5% for payment within 14 days. The invoice was settled by cheque five days later. The entries required to record BOTH of these transactions are:

		Debit £	*Credit* £
A	PQ Limited	640	
	Sales		640
	Bank	608	
	Discount allowed	32	
	PQ Limited		640

		Debit £	*Credit* £
B	PQ Limited	640	
	Sales		640
	Bank	600	
	Discount allowed	40	
	PQ Limited		640

		Debit £	*Credit* £
C	PQ Limited	640	
	Sales		640
	Bank	608	
	Discount received	32	
	PQ Limited		640

		Debit £	*Credit* £
D	PQ Limited	800	
	Sales		800
	Bank	608	
	Discount allowed	182	
	PQ Limited		800

---

22 A fixed asset was purchased at the beginning of Year 1 for £2,400 and depreciated by 20% per annum by the reducing balance method. At the beginning of Year 4 it was sold for £1,200. The result of this was:

A a loss on disposal of £240.00

B a loss on disposal of £28.80

C a profit on disposal of £28.80

D a profit on disposal of £240.00

---

23 Your organisation uses the Weighted Average Cost method of valuing stocks. During August 1997, the following stock details were recorded:

Opening balance	30 units valued at £2 each
5 August	purchase of 50 units at £2.40 each
10 August	issue of 40 units
18 August	purchase of 60 units at £2.50 each
23 August	issue of 25 units

The value of the balance at 31 August 1997 was:

A £172.50

B £176.25

C £180.00

D £187.50

---

24 During September, your organisation had sales of £148,000 which made a gross profit of £40,000. Purchases amounted to £100,000 and opening stock was £34,000.

The value of closing stock was:

A £24,000

B £26,000

C £42,000

D £54,000

---

25 During the year ended 31 October 1997, your organisation made a gross profit of £60,000 which represented a mark-up of 50%. Opening stock was £12,000 and closing stock was £18,000.

The rate of stock turnover was:

A 4 times

B 6.7 times

C 7.3 times

D 8 times

---

26 The responsibility for ensuring that all accounting transactions are properly recorded and summarised in the final accounts lies with:

A the external auditors

B the internal auditors

C the shareholders

D the directors

---

27 Sales revenue should be recognised when goods and services have been supplied; costs are incurred when goods and services have been received.

The accounting concept which governs the above is the:

A going concern concept

B materiality concept

C realisation concept

D dual aspect concept

---

28 The capital maintenance concept implies that:

A the capital of a business should be kept intact by not paying out dividends

B a business should invest its profits in the purchase of capital assets

C fixed assets should be properly maintained

D profit is earned only if the value of an organisation's net assets or its operating capability has increased during the accounting period

---

29 The following totals appear in the day books for March 1998:

	Goods excluding VAT £	*VAT* £
Sales day book	40,000	7,000
Purchases day book	20,000	3,500
Returns inwards day book	2,000	350
Returns outwards day book	4,000	700

Opening and closing stocks are both £3,000. The gross profit for March 1998 is:

A £18,000

B £21,150

C £22,000

D £25,850

---

30 Your firm's cash book at 30 April 1998 shows a balance at the bank of £2,490. Comparison with the bank statement at the same date reveals the following differences:

	£
Unpresented cheques	840
Bank charges not in cash book	50
Receipts not yet credited by the bank	470
Dishonoured cheque not in cash book	140

The correct bank balance at 30 April 1998 is:

A £1,460

B £2,300

C £2,580

D £3,140

---

31 A business' bank balance increased by £750,000 during its last financial year. During the same period it issued shares of £1 million and repaid a debenture of £750,000. It purchased fixed assets for £200,000 and charged depreciation of £100,000. Working capital (other than the bank balance) increased by £575,000.

Its profit for the year was:

A £1,175,000

B £1,275,000

C £1,325,000

D £1,375,00

---

32 The record of how the profit or loss of a company has been allocated to distributions and reserves is found in the:

A capital account

B profit and loss account

C reserves account

D appropriation account

---

33 A sole trader's business made a profit of £32,500 during the year ended 31 March 1998. This figure was after deducting £100 per week wages for himself. In addition, he put his home telephone bill through the business books, amounting to £400 plus VAT at 17.5%. He is registered for VAT and therefore has charged only the net amount to his profit and loss account.

His capital at 1 April 1997 was £6,500. His capital at 31 March 1998 was:

A £33,730

B £33,800

C £38,930

D £39,000

---

34 A business incurs expenditure on the following research and development activities:

£120,000 on pure research
£200,000 on applied research
£350,000 on product development

The amount which could be capitalised is:

A nil

B £350,000

C £550,000

D £670,000

---

35 A business has the following trading account for the year ending 31 May 1998:

	£	£
Sales turnover		45,000
Opening stock	4,000	
Purchases	26,500	
	30,500	
Less: Closing stock	6,000	
		24,500
Gross profit		20,500

Its rate of stock turnover for the year is:

A 4.9 times

B 5.3 times

C 7.5 times

D 9 times

---

36 A company's gearing ratio would rise if:

A a decrease in long-term loans is LESS than a decrease in shareholders' funds

B a decrease in long-term loans is MORE than a decrease in shareholders' funds

C interest rates rose

D dividends were paid

---

37 A company has the following details extracted from its balance sheet:

	£000
Stocks	1,900
Debtors	1,000
Bank overdraft	100
Creditors	1,000

Its liquidity position could be said to be:

A very well controlled because its current assets far outweigh its current liabilities

B poorly controlled because its quick assets are less than its current liabilities

C poorly controlled because its current ratio is significantly higher than the industry norm of 1.8

D poorly controlled because it has a bank overdraft

---

38 The gross profit mark-up is 40% where:

A sales are £120,000 and gross profit is £48,000

B sales are £120,000 and cost of sales is £72,000

C sales are £100,800 and cost of sales is £72,000

D sales are £100,800 and cost of sales is £60,480

---

39 Revenue reserves would decrease if a company:

A sets aside profits to pay future dividends

B transfers amounts into 'general reserves'

C issues shares at a premium

D pays dividends

---

40 Your purchase ledger control account has a balance at 1 October 1998 of £34,500 credit. During October, credit purchases were £78,400, cash purchases were £2,400 and payments made to suppliers, excluding cash purchases and after deducting cash discounts of £1,200, were £68,900. Purchase returns were £4,700.

The closing balance was:

A £38,100

B £40,500

C £47,500

D £49,900

---

41 Diesel fuel in stock at 1 November 1997 was £12,500 and there were invoices awaited for £1,700. During the year to 31 October 1998, diesel fuel bills of £85,400 were paid and a delivery worth £1,300 had yet to be invoiced. At 31 October 1998, the stock of diesel fuel was valued at £9,800. The diesel fuel to be charged to the profit and loss account for the year to 31 October 1998 is:

A £85,100

B £87,700

C £88,500

D £91,100

---

42 Your firm values stock using the weighted average cost method. At 1 October 1998, there were 60 units in stock valued at £12 each. On 8 October, 40 units were purchased for £15 each and a further 50 units were purchased for £18 each on 14 October. On 21 October, 75 units were sold for £1,200.

The value of closing stock at 31 October 1998 was:

A £900

B £1,020

C £1,110

D £1,125

---

43 A machine cost £9,000. It has an expected useful life of 6 years, and an expected residual value of £1,000. It is to be depreciated at 30% per annum on the reducing balance basis. A full year's depreciation is charged in the year of purchase, with none in the year of sale. During year 4, it is sold for £3,000.

The profit or loss on disposal is:

A loss £87

B loss £2,000

C profit £256

D profit £1,200

---

44 An increase in the provision for doubtful debts results in:

A a decrease in current liabilities

B an increase in net profit

C an increase in working capital

D a decrease in working capital

---

45 The most appropriate definition of depreciation is:

A a means of determining the decrease in market value of an asset over time

B a means of allocating the cost of an asset over a number of accounting periods

C a means of setting funds aside for the replacement of the asset

D a means of estimating the current value of the asset

---

46 A company has the following current assets and liabilities at 31 October 1998:

		£
Current assets:	stock	970
	debtors	380
	bank	40
		1,390
Current liabilities:	creditors	420

When measured against accepted 'norms', the company can be said to have:

A a high current ratio and an ideal acid test ratio

B an ideal current ratio and a low acid test ratio

C a high current ratio and a low acid test ratio

D ideal current and acid test ratios

---

47 Your company's profit and loss account for the year ended 30 September 1998 showed the following:

	£000
Net profit before interest and tax	1,200
Interest	200
	1,000
Corporation tax	400
Retained profit for the year	600

Its balance sheet at 30 September 1997 showed the following capital:

	£000
Share capital	8,000
Profit and loss account balance	1,200
	9,200
10% debenture	2,000
	11,200

Return on average capital employed for the year ended 30 September 1998 is:

A 5.88%

B 10.17%

C 10.43%

D none of these

---

48 An increase in both debtors' and creditors' payment periods could result in:

A an increase in working capital

B a decrease in working capital

C an increase in current assets and current liabilities

D a decrease in current assets and current liabilities

---

49 In times of rising prices, the historical cost convention:

A understates asset values and profits

B understates asset values and overstates profits

C overstates asset values and profits

D overstates asset values and understates profits

---

50 The main aim of financial accounting is to:

A record all transactions in the books of account

B provide management with detailed analyses of costs

C present the financial results of the organisation by means of recognised statements

D calculate profit

---

51 The accounting concept which dictates that fixed assets should be valued at cost, less accumulated depreciation, rather than their enforced saleable value, is the:

A net realisable value concept

B prudence concept

C realisation concept

D going concern concept

---

52 Your firm's bank statement at 31 October 1998 shows a balance of £13,400. You subsequently discover that the bank has dishonoured a customer's cheque for £300 and has charged bank charges of £50, neither of which is recorded in your cash book. There are unpresented cheques totalling £1,400. You further discover that an automatic receipt from a customer of £195 has been recorded as a credit in your cash book.

Your cash book balance, prior to correcting the errors and omissions, was:

A £11,455

B £11,960

C £12,000

D £12,155

---

53 Financial accounts differ from management accounts in that they:

A are prepared monthly for internal control purposes

B contain details of costs incurred in manufacturing

C are summarised and prepared mainly for external users of accounting information

D provide information to enable the trial balance to be prepared

---

54 The petty cash imprest is restored to £100 at the end of each week. The following amounts are paid out of petty cash during week 23:

Stationery	£14.10	including VAT at 17.5%
Travelling costs	£25.50	
Office refreshments	£12.90	
Sundry creditors	£24.00	plus VAT at 17.5%

The amount required to restore the imprest to £100 is:

A £19.30

B £25.60

C £74.40

D £80.70

---

55 Your firm's cash book shows a credit bank balance of £1,240 at 30 April 1999. Upon comparison with the bank statement, you determine that there are unpresented cheques totalling £450, and a receipt of £140 which has not yet been passed through the bank account. The bank statement shows bank charges of £75 which have not been entered in the cash book.

The balance on the bank statement is:

A £1,005 overdrawn

B £930 overdrawn

C £1,475

D £1,550

---

56 Which ONE of the following is an error of principle?

A A gas bill credited to the gas account and debited to the bank account

B The purchase of a fixed asset credited to the asset at cost account and debited to the creditor's account

C The purchase of a fixed asset debited to the purchases account and credited to the creditor's account

D The payment of wages debited and credited to the correct accounts, but using the wrong amount

---

57 A fixed asset was disposed of for £2,200 during the last accounting year. It had been purchased exactly three years earlier for £5,000 with an expected residual value of £500, and had been depreciated on the reducing balance basis, at 20% per annum.

The profit or loss on disposal was:

A £360 loss

B £150 loss

C £104 loss

D £200 profit

---

58 Stock movements for product X during the last quarter were as follows:

January	Purchases	10 items at £19.80 each
February	Sales	10 items at £30 each
March	Purchases	20 items at £24.50 each
	Sales	5 items at £30 each

Opening stock at 1 January was 6 items valued at £15 each.

Gross profit for the quarter, using the weighted average cost method, would be:

A £135.75

B £155.00

C £174.00

D £483.00

---

59 A computerised accounts package would be MOST useful in maintaining:

A the ledger accounts

B the books of prime entry

C a register of fixed assets

D the stock records

---

60 An error of original entry would occur if the purchase of goods for resale was:

A debited and credited to the correct accounts using the incorrect amount in both cases

B credited to the purchases account and debited to the supplier's account

C debited to a fixed assets account

D entered correctly to the purchases account, but entered in the supplier's account using the wrong amount

---

61 The reducing balance method of depreciating fixed assets is more appropriate than the straight-line method when:

A there is no expected residual value for the asset

B the expected life of the asset is not capable of being estimated

C the asset is expected to be replaced in a short period of time

D the asset is consumed less in later years than in the early years of use.

---

62 Your organisation has received a statement of account from one of its suppliers, showing an outstanding balance due to them of £1,350. On comparison with your ledger account, the following is determined:

- your ledger account shows a credit balance of £260
- the supplier has disallowed cash discount of £80 due to late payment of an invoice
- the supplier has not yet allowed for goods returned at the end of the period of £270
- cash in transit of £830 has not been received by the supplier

Following consideration of these items, the unreconciled difference between the two records is:

A £70

B £90

C £430

D £590

---

63 A cash flow statement can BEST be described as:

A a statement showing the effects of profit on cash resources

B a statement of cash inflows and outflows from operating activities

C a statement showing the movement in working capital

D a statement showing all the inflows and outflows of cash

---

64 Your organisation's trial balance at 31 October 1999 is out of agreement, with the debit side totalling £500 less than the credit side. During November, the following errors are discovered:

- the sales journal for October had been undercast by £150
- rent received of £240 had been credited to the rent payable account
- the provision for bad debts, which decreased by £420, had been recorded in the provision for bad debts account as an increase

Following the correction of these errors, the balance on the suspense account would be:

A Credit £190

B Credit £670

C Credit £1,190

D Debit £1,490

---

65 On 1 November 1999, your organisation purchased, on credit from XYZ Limited, office equipment with a catalogue price of £1,000 less trade discount of 20% and cash discount of 5%, if paid for within 14 days. The correct journal entry to record the purchase on 1 November 1999 (ignoring VAT) is:

		Debit £	*Credit* £
A	Office equipment	1,000	
	XYZ Limited		750
	Discount received		250
B	Office equipment	1,000	
	XYZ Limited		760
	Discount received		240
C	Office equipment	800	
	XYZ Limited		800
D	Office equipment	800	
	XYZ Limited		760
	Discount received		40

---

66 The following sales ledger control account contains some entries which have been posted to the wrong side of the account.

Sales ledger control account

	£		£
Opening debtors	14,500	Credit sales	53,500
Discounts allowed	350	Returns	1,400
Receipts from debtors	51,200	Contra to purchase ledger	500

The correct closing debtors figure should be:

A £12,750

B £14,550

C £15,250

D £15,550

---

67 An increase in the gross profit margin of a business is most likely to be due to which ONE of the following combinations:

	Selling price per unit	*Quantity sold*	*Cost per unit*
A	increased	no change	increased
B	no change	increased	no change
C	no change	no change	decreased
D	decreased	increased	increased

---

68 A business has the following capital and long-term liabilities:

	31.10.98 *£m*	*31.10.99* *£m*
12% debentures	20	40
Issued share capital	15	30
Share premium	3	18
Retained profits	22	12

At 31 October 1999, its gearing ratio, compared to that at 31 October 1998, has:

A risen, resulting in greater risk for shareholders

B risen, resulting in greater security for shareholders

C fallen, resulting in greater security for shareholders

D remained the same

---

69 A business has the following trading accounts:

	Year ended 31 October 1998		*Year ended 31 October 1999*	
	£000	*£000*	*£000*	*£000*
Sales		2,000		2,650
Less: Cost of sales				
Opening stock	75		85	
Purchases	1,260		1,330	
	1,335		1,415	
Less: Closing stock	85		115	
		1,250		1,300
Gross profit		750		1,350

During the year ended 31 October 1999, its rate of stock turnover, compared with that for the year ended 31 October 1998, has:

A decreased, with a possible beneficial effect on liquidity

B decreased, with a possible detrimental effect on liquidity

C increased, with a possible detrimental effect on liquidity

D increased, with a possible beneficial effect on liquidity

---

70 Stocks should be valued at the lower of cost and net realisable value. Which ONE of the following accounting concepts governs this?

A the consistency concept

B the accruals concept

C the prudence concept

D the money measurement concept

---

71 The historical cost concept:

A records transactions from past years

B fails to take account of changing price levels over time

C values assets at their cost to the business, irrespective of any depreciation or other loss in value

D is no longer used in modern accounting systems

---

72 By charging depreciation in the accounts, a business aims to ensure that:

A the cost of fixed assets is spread over the accounting periods which benefit from their use

B there are sufficient funds set aside to replace the assets when necessary

C its profits are not understated

D the assets are shown at their real value

---

73 A sales ledger control account showed a debit balance of £37,642. The individual debtors' accounts in the sales ledger showed a total of £35,840. The difference could be due to:

A undercasting the sales day book by £1,802

B overcasting the sales returns day book by £1,802

C entering a cash receipt of £1,802 on the debit side of a debtor's account

D entering cash discount allowed of £901 on the debit side of the control account

---

74 A debit balance of £1,250 on X's account in the books of Y meant that:

A X owes £1,250 to Y

B Y owes £1,250 to X

C X has returned goods worth £1,250 to Y

D X is owed £1,250 by Y

---

75 A machine was purchased in 1996 for £64,000. It was expected to last for 5 years and to have a residual value of £2,000. Depreciation was charged at 50% per annum on the reducing balance basis, with a full year's charge in the year of purchase. No depreciation is charged in the year of disposal. The company's year end is 31 December. The machine was sold on 3 April 2000 for £2,500. The profit or loss on sale is:

A profit £500

B profit £562.50

C loss £1,375

D loss £1,500

---

76 A true and fair view is given by the accounts when:

A assets are stated at their true values in the balance sheet

B they have been audited and found to be accurate

C they fairly reflect the financial position of an organisation, sufficient for users of the accounts to make proper judgements

D the auditors are able to certify that they contain no errors or omissions, and that no fraud has been committed

---

77 A company's telephone bill consists of two elements. One is a quarterly rental charge, payable in advance; the other is a quarterly charge for calls made, payable in arrears. At 1 April 1999, the previous bill dated 1 March 1999 had included line rental of £90. Estimated call charges during March 1999 were £80.

During the following 12 months, bills totalling £2,145 were received on 1 June, 1 September, 1 December and 1 March 2000, each containing rental of £90 as well as call charges. Estimated call charges during March 2000 were £120.

The amount to be charged to the profit and loss account for the year ended 31 March 2000 in respect of telephone costs is:

A £2,145

B £2,185

C £2,205

D £2,234

---

78 A sole trader had net assets of £19,000 at 30 April 2000. During the year to 30 April 2000, he introduced £9,800 additional capital into the business. Profits were £8,000, of which he withdrew £4,200. His capital at 1 May 1999 was:

A £3,000

B £5,400

C £13,000

D £16,600

---

79 A company made a profit for the year of £18,750, after accounting for depreciation of £1,250. During the year, fixed assets were purchased for £8,000, debtors increased by £1,000, stocks decreased by £1,800 and creditors increased by £350.

The increase in cash and bank balances during the year was:

A £10,650

B £10,850

C £12,450

D £13,150

---

80 In times of rising prices, the valuation of stock using the First In First Out method, as opposed to the Weighted Average Cost method, will result in which ONE of the following combinations?

	Cost of sales	*Profit*	*Closing stock*
A	Lower	Higher	Higher
B	Lower	Higher	Lower
C	Higher	Lower	Higher
D	Higher	Higher	Lower

---

81 A company had the following gross profit calculation in its last accounting period:

	£
Sales	130,000
Cost of sales	60,000
Gross profit	70,000

Average stock during that period was £7,500.

In the next accounting period, sales are expected to increase by 40%, and the rate of stock turnover is expected to double. If average stock remains at £7,500 the gross profit mark-up percentage will be:

A 30.0%

B 34.1%

C 51.7%

D 65.9%

---

82 In 1999, a company's current ratio was 2.5 : 1 and its acid test ratio was 0.8 : 1. By the end of 2000, the ratios are expected to be 3 : 1 and 0.6 : 1 respectively. These changes are most likely to be due to which ONE of the following?

A increased bank balances

B decreased bank balances

C increased stocks

D increased debtors and creditors

Questions

Question 1

Statement of Principles

The UK Accounting Standards Board (ASB) has issued a Statement of Principles.

Required

(a) What is the purpose of the Statement of Principles? **(5 marks)**

(b) Explain the following qualitative characteristics of financial information:

(i) Materiality

(ii) Relevance

(iii) Reliability **(5 marks)**

(Total : 10 marks)

Question 2

User groups

(a) Outline the information needs of the following groups of users of financial statements:

- Shareholders
- Management
- Employees **(5 marks)**

(b) Explain the extent to which a company's published financial statements are useful to each of the above user groups. **(5 marks)**

(Total : 10 marks)

Question 3

Owner of a business (ACCA 12/00)

The owner of a business may choose to run it as a sole trader or as a limited liability company.

Required

Explain five differences between the two methods of operation.

(Total : 10 marks)

Question 4

Historical cost accounting (ACCA 12/97)

Historical cost accounting has been the normal method of accounting in most countries for many years.

Required

Explain four respects in which the use of historical cost accounting may distort financial statements or their interpretation.

(Total : 10 marks)

Question 5

Limitations of HCA (ACCA 12/97)

Give four reasons why historical cost accounting continues in use as the normal method of accounting, despite its limitations.

(Total : 10 marks)

Question 6

Accounting concepts (ACCA 12/97 amended)

Accounting practice depends upon the guidance provided by a number of accounting concepts, some of which are to be found in FRS 18 *Accounting Policies* which superseded SSAP 2 *Disclosure of Accounting Policies* and/or in the *Statement of Principles for Financial Reporting* produced by the UK Accounting Standards Board.

Required

Define and explain the relevance of the following accounting concepts:

(i) Neutrality

(ii) Money measurement

(iii) Accruals

(iv) Substance over form

(v) Consistency

(Total : 10 marks)

Question 7

Conflict of concepts

Give two examples of situations in which there is a clash or inconsistency between two accounting concepts or conventions, and explain how the inconsistency should be resolved.

(Total : 10 marks)

Question 8

Ermine (ACCA 12/99)

Ermine commenced trading on 1 July 20X8 with a capital of £100,000 cash. During the year ended 30 June 20X9, he operated from rented premises and at the end of the year he had sold all his stock. His balance sheet at 30 June 20X9 was:

	£	£
Cash at bank		100,000
		100,000
Capital at 1 July 20X8	100,000	
Profit for year to date	40,000	
	140,000	
Less: Drawings	40,000	
		100,000
		100,000

During the year there was inflation of 10% in the country in which he operates.

Required

Using this simple example where appropriate, define the terms *financial capital* and *physical capital*, and explain why it may be dangerous for an enterprise if it maintains financial capital but does not maintain physical capital.

(Total : 10 marks)

Question 9

HCA (ACCA 12/99)

(a) List and briefly explain *three* ways in which the use of historical cost accounting may cause financial statements to be misleading. **(6 marks)**

(b) List *three* advantages of historical cost accounting. **(4 marks)**

(Total : 10 marks)

Question 10

Concepts (ACCA 6/00)

Define the following accounting concepts and give for each one an example of its application:

(a) Money measurement **(2 marks)**

(b) Substance over form **(2 marks)**

(c) Consistency (see note below) **(2 marks)**

(d) Duality **(2 marks)**

(e) Prudence **(2 marks)**

Note: Your answer to (c) should include a brief explanation of the circumstances in which the consistency concept should not be applied.

(Total : 10 marks)

Question 11

Turner (ACCA 12/98)

The bookkeeping system of Turner Limited is not computerised, and at 30 September 20X8 the bookkeeper was unable to balance the accounts.

The trial balance totals were as follows.

Debit	£1,796,100
Credit	£1,852,817

He nevertheless proceeded to prepare draft financial statements, inserting the difference as a balancing figure in the balance sheet.

He then opened a suspense account for the difference and began to check through the accounting records to find the difference. He found the following errors and omissions.

(i) £8,980, the total of the sales returns book for September 20X8, had been credited to purchases returns account.

(ii) £9,600 paid for an item of plant purchased on 1 April 20X8 had been debited to plant repairs account. The company depreciates its plant at 20% per annum on the straight line basis, with proportional depreciation in the year of purchase.

(iii) The cash discount totals for the month of September 20X8 had not been posted to the nominal ledger accounts. The figures were as follows.

Discount allowed	£836
Discount received	£919

(iv) £580 insurance prepaid at 30 September 20X7 had not been brought down as an opening balance.

(v) The balance of £38,260 on the telephone expense account had been omitted from the trial balance.

(vi) A car held as a fixed asset had been sold during the year for £4,800. The proceeds of sale were entered in the cash book but had been credited to sales account in the nominal ledger. The original cost of the car, £12,000, and the accumulated depreciation to date £8,000, were included in the motor vehicles account and the accumulated depreciation account. The company depreciates motor vehicles at 25% per annum on the straight line basis with proportionate depreciation in the year of purchase, but none in the year of sale.

Required

Open a suspense account for the difference between the trial balance totals. Prepare the journal entries necessary to correct the errors and eliminate the balance on the suspense account. Narratives are not required.

(Total : 10 marks)

Question 12

Rook (ACCA 6/00)

The following transactions of Rook Limited took place in the year ended 31 March 20X0:

(a) The clearance of a difference in the trial balance for which a suspense account had been opened. The difference was found to be caused by a £2,000 under-statement of the debit side of the salaries account in the nominal ledger.

(1 mark)

(b) The acceptance of a car worth £6,000 in settlement of a sales ledger debt of £7,500 due from Wren Limited. No other money will be received from Wren Limited. The car is to be used by one of the sales representatives of Rook Limited. **(1 mark)**

(c) The construction of an extension to Rook's factory using materials from stock and the company's own labour force. The costs were:

Materials taken from stock	£27,600
Labour	£18,500

(2 marks)

(d) Rook Limited purchased a number of assets from Crow Limited. It was agreed that the total purchase price was not to be paid immediately but was to remain as a loan to be repaid by Rook over several years. The assets purchased were:

	£
Motor vehicles	18,000
Plant and machinery	33,000
Goods for resale in the normal course of Rook's business	20,000
	£71,000

(2 marks)

(e) The purchase of a car from Car Dealer for £20,000 on 19 March 20X0. On that date, Rook Limited gave in part exchange a vehicle which had cost £18,000 and which had a written down value of £12,000. The agreed part exchange value of this vehicle was its written down value £12,000. The balance of £8,000 is to be paid on 30 April 20X0.

(4 marks)

Required

Show journal entries, with narrations, to record these transactions. Note that entries to ledger control accounts are not required for item (b).

(Total : 10 marks)

Question 13

MLN

The trial balance of MLN plc was extracted on 30 September 20X9 and showed the following totals.

Debit	£1,605,668	Credit	£1,603,623

A suspense account was opened and used to record the difference until it could be investigated but the company continued its draft accounts by applying the prudence concept to the treatment of the suspense account balance.

After investigation the following facts emerged.

(1) Discounts allowed of £1,248 had not been entered in the sales ledger control account.

(2) A credit sale of £857 to SEC Ltd had not been entered in the sales day book.

(3) A contra entry between the sales and purchase ledgers had been entered in the control accounts as:

Debit sales ledger control	£731
Credit purchase ledger control	£731

(4) A telephone bill of £54 for telephones had been entered in the telephone expense account as £45 but was correctly entered in the creditor's account.

(5) Bank charges of £66 has been correctly entered in the expense account but had not been entered in the cash book.

(6) One of the pages of the purchase day book had been incorrectly totalled as £11,269 instead of £11,629.

(7) During the year a fixed asset was sold for £740. Its original cost was £3,600 and its net book value at the date of disposal was £800. The only entry made was to debit the proceeds of sale to the bank account.

Required

(a) Record in the suspense account the effects of correcting (1) to (7) above.

(3 marks)

(b) Reconcile the difference between the balance on the sales ledger control account in the original trial balance and the sum of the individual customer balances in the sales ledger. The original control account balance was £327,762.

(4 marks)

(c) Prepare a statement of adjusted net profit showing both the original net profit of £412,967 as given by the draft accounts and the net profit after correcting items (1) to (7) above. **(3 marks)**

(Total : 10 marks)

Question 14

YTZ

When the trial balance of YTZ Ltd was extracted on 30 June 20X2 it showed the following totals.

Dr	*Cr*
£	£
103,457	102,113

At the time a suspense account was opened to record the difference but investigation has now followed and the following facts have emerged.

(1) An invoice for travel expenses of £132 was entered in the travel expenses account as £123, although correctly entered in the creditor's account.

(2) The returns outwards book was undercast on one page by £100.

(3) An electricity bill for £154 that had not been recorded or accrued for was discovered.

(4) Discounts received of £1,870 had not been entered in the purchase ledger control account.

(5) The bank statement that has recently been received showed an amount of interest on the overdraft of £28 which has not been recorded in the ledgers.

(6) A small item of machinery costing £1,450 was charged to the repairs account. Depreciation is charged on machinery at the rate of 20% per annum on cost.

(7) Discounts allowed of £30 were not recorded in the cash received book.

(8) A settlement by contra entry of £3,200 was only recorded in the purchase ledger control account.

(9) Bank charges of £23 had been correctly entered in the expense account but not in the cash book.

Required

(a) Clear the suspense account balance by correcting each of the errors detailed above. **(4 marks)**

(b) Prepare a statement of adjusted profit showing the original profit of £97,499 and the net profit after correcting the items above. **(6 marks)**

(Total : 10 marks)

Question 15

Provision (ACCA 12/93)

The balance on the provision for doubtful debts account on 1 January 20X1 was £1,000, equal to 5% of debtors at that date.

In the 12 months to 31 December 20X1 sales are £90,000, cash receipts from sales are £80,000 and bad debts (charged to the provision account) are £600. The doubtful debts provision balance at close of business on 31 December 20X1 is required to be 5% of debtors.

In the 12 months to 31 December 20X2 sales are £100,000, cash receipts from sales are £110,000 and bad debts (charged directly to expenses) are £400. The doubtful debts provision balance at close of business on 31 December 20X2 is required to be 5% of debtors. (The change in treatment of bad debts in the second year does not imply that an adjustment or correction should be made in relation to the first year.)

Required

(a) Prepare the provision for doubtful debts account for the period 1 January 20X1 to 1 January 20X3, clearly bringing down the balance at the end of each year, and indicating the double entry for each item in the account. Submit necessary workings in a convenient form. **(5 marks)**

(b) Is the balance on the provision for doubtful debts account a liability? Explain your answer briefly but clearly. **(5 marks)**

(Total : 10 marks)

Question 16

Wholesalers

On 1 January 20X1 the accounting records of Wholesalers plc included the following balances. All figures are in £000.

		£
Sales ledger control account		50
Provision for doubtful debts		2
Individual sales ledger memorandum balances		
- positive/(negative)	A	10
	B	20
	C	8
	D	9
	E	6
	F	(2)
	G	(1)

The following unaudited information is presented to you concerning the year 20X1.

Sales day book		*Cash book receipts*		
Customer	*Amount*	*Customer*	*Amount*	*Discount*
	£		£	£
A	30	A	35	2
B	35	B	30	
D	18	C	5	
E	9	D	20	
F	8	E	12	
G	7	F	5	1
		G	4	
	117		111	3

Sales return book		*Bad debts written off*	
Customer	*Amount*	*Customer*	*Amount*
	£		£
A	2	C	2
F	3		
	5		2

Contra with creditors ledger

Customer	*Amount*
	£
E	2
G	4
	6

At 31 December 20X1, C's debt should be provided against in full and the general provision should be 4% of remaining debtors.

Required

Prepare a sales ledger control account, provision for doubtful debts account, and sales ledger accounts for each customer, for the year 20X1. Carry down year-end balances and prove that the sales ledger control balances reconciles with the memorandum balances. The ledger accounts may be presented in any summarised form you find convenient.

(Total : 10 marks)

Question 17

Averill

Averill Ltd had the following balances on its motor vehicles accounts at 30 September 20X2.

	£
Motor vehicles at cost	10,000
Provision for depreciation of motor vehicles	4,000

During the year to 30 September 20X3, the following transactions occurred.

31 January 20X3	Bought a motor van (plant number MV11) costing £9,000.
24 April 20X3	Sold a motor van (plant number MV05) for £500 which had originally cost £4,000 in January 20X0.

During the year to 30 September 20X4, the following transactions occurred.

20 February 20X4	Bought a motor van (plant number MV12) costing £12,000.
31 August 20X4	Traded-in van bought on 31 January 20X3 (plant number MV11) for a new van (plant number MV13) costing £14,000. The trade-in allowance was £7,400.

Averill Ltd provides for depreciation on its motor vehicles at a rate of 25% per annum using the reducing balance method. It is company policy to make a full year's charge against all assets held at the end of its financial year (30 September).

Required

Show the ledger accounts necessary to record the above transactions. The form of presentation should clearly show the values which will be transferred to the company's profit and loss account and balance sheet at the end of *each* of the financial years to 30 September 20X3 and 20X4.

(Total : 10 marks)

Question 18

Diamond (ACCA 6/97)

Diamond plc is a trading company making up its accounts regularly to 31 December each year.

At 1 January 20X5 the following balances existed in the records of Diamond plc.

	£000
Freehold land - cost	1,000
Freehold buildings - cost	500
Aggregate depreciation provided on buildings to 31 December 20X4	210
Office equipment - cost	40
Aggregate depreciation provided on office equipment to 31 December 20X4	24

The company's depreciation policies are as follows:

- Freehold land - no depreciation.
- Freehold buildings - depreciation provided at 2% per annum on cost on the straight line basis.
- Office equipment - depreciation provided at 12½% per annum on the straight line basis.
- A full year's depreciation is charged in the year of acquisition of all assets and none in the year of disposal.

During the two years to 31 December 20X6 the following transactions took place.

Year ended 31 December 20X5

10 June	Office equipment purchased for £16,000. This equipment was to replace some old items which were given in part exchange. Their agreed part exchange value was £4,000. They had originally cost £8,000 and their book value was £1,000. The company paid the balance of £12,000 in cash.
08 October	An extension was made to the building at a cost of £50,000.

Year ended 31 December 20X6

1 March	Office equipment which had cost £8,000 and with a written down value of £2,000 was sold for £3,000.

In preparing the financial statements at 31 December 20X6 it was decided to revalue the land upwards by £200,000 to reflect a recent survey.

Required

Write up the necessary ledger accounts to record these transactions for the *two* years ended 31 December 20X6. Separate cost (or valuation) and aggregate depreciation accounts are required; you should *not* combine cost and depreciation in a single account.

(Total : 10 marks)

Question 19

FRS 15

Explain the purpose of depreciation according to FRS 15 *Tangible Fixed Assets*, and the factors which should be taken into account in assessing the amount of depreciation required each year.

(Total : 10 marks)

Question 20

Stoat (ACCA 12/99)

The directors of Stoat Limited are reviewing the company's draft financial statements for the year ended 30 June 20X9.

Two matters under discussion are depreciation and fixed asset valuation – several directors are of the opinion that the company's depreciation methods and rates are unsatisfactory, and that the balance sheet values of some of the fixed assets are unrealistic.

Required

Draft a memorandum for the directors dealing with the following matters:

(a) Three items of evidence obtainable from inside or outside the company, to check whether the company's depreciation rates are in fact likely to be too low.

(3 marks)

(b) The disclosures, if any, which would be required in the financial statements if the company decided to change its depreciation methods. **(3 marks)**

(c) The requirements of FRS 15 and the Companies Acts regarding revaluation of fixed assets. **(4 marks)**

(Total : 10 marks)

Question 21

Pentland (ACCA 12/00)

Pentland Limited compiles its financial statements for the year to 30 June each year.

At 1 July 20X0 the company's balance sheet included the following figures:

	Cost	*Accumulated depreciation*	*Net book value*
	£000	*£000*	*£000*
Land	4,000	Nil	4,000
Buildings	2,200	800	1,400
Motor vehicles	600	200	400

Depreciation is charged at the following annual rates (all straight line):

Land	Nil
Buildings	2%
Motor vehicles	20%

A proportionate depreciation charge is made in the year of purchase, sale or revaluation of an asset.

During the year ended 30 June 20X1 the following transactions took place:

(1) 1 January 20X1 — The company decided to adopt a policy of revaluing its buildings and they were revalued to £3.4m.

(2) 1 April 20X1 — A new motor vehicle was purchased for £30,000. Part of the purchase price was settled by part exchanging another motor vehicle, which had cost £20,000, at an agreed value of £12,000. The balance of £18,000 was paid in cash.

The motor vehicle given in part-exchange had a net book value (cost less depreciation) at 30 June 20X0 of £10,000.

Required

Prepare ledger accounts to record these transactions in the records of Pentland Limited.

(Total : 10 marks)

Question 22

Cost and NRV

'The idea that stock should be included in accounts at the lower of historical cost and net realisable value follows the prudence convention but not the consistency convention.'

(a) Explain clearly what is meant by the following terms.

(i) Historical cost
(ii) Net realisable value
(iii) Prudence convention
(iv) Consistency convention **(5 marks)**

(b) Do you agree with the quotation? **(2 marks)**

(c) Explain, with reasons, whether you think this idea (that stocks should be included in accounts at the lower of historical cost and net realisable value) is a useful one. Refer to at least two classes of user of financial accounting reports in your answer. **(3 marks)**

(Total : 10 marks)

Question 23

SSAP 9 (ACCA 6/98)

SSAP 9 *Stocks and Long-term Contracts* requires stocks of raw materials and finished goods to be valued in financial statements at the lower of cost and net realisable value.

Required

(a) Appendix 1 to SSAP 9 states that in arriving at the cost of stock, methods such as last in first out (LIFO) are not usually appropriate. Explain how LIFO is applied. **(2 marks)**

(b) Describe three methods of arriving at cost of stock which are acceptable under SSAP 9 and explain why they are regarded as acceptable, and LIFO is not. **(5 marks)**

(c) Explain how the cost of a stock of finished goods held by the manufacturer would normally be arrived at when obtaining the figure for the financial statements. **(3 marks)**

(Total : 10 marks)

Question 24

Sampi (ACCA 6/98)

Sampi is a manufacturer of garden furniture. The company has consistently used FIFO (first in first out) in valuing stock, but it is interested to know the effect on its stock valuation of using LIFO (last in first out) and weighted average cost instead of FIFO.

At 28 February 20X8 the company had a stock of 4,000 standard plastic tables, and has computed its value on each of the three bases as follows.

Basis	*Unit cost*	*Total value*
	£	£
FIFO	16	64,000
LIFO	12	48,000
Weighted average	13	52,000

During March 20X8 the movements on the stock of tables were as follows.

Received from factory:

Date	*Number of units*	*Production cost per unit*
		£
8 March	3,800	15
22 March	6,000	18

Sales:

Date	*Number of units*
12 March	5,000
18 March	2,000
24 March	3,000
28 March	2,000

On a FIFO basis the stock at 31 March 20X8 was £32,400.

Required

Compute what the value of the stock at 31 March 20X8 would be using each of the following bases.

(a) LIFO **(5 marks)**

(b) Weighted average cost **(5 marks)**

In arriving at the total stock values you should make calculations to two decimal places (where necessary) and deal with each stock movement in date order.

(Total : 10 marks)

Question 25

Journals

A company maintains a debtors control account in the nominal ledger, and includes the balance on this account in its trial balance. It also maintains a memorandum individual debtors ledger.

The following errors relating to debtors have been discovered.

(a) A credit note for £90 had been entered as if it were an invoice.

(b) Sales of £400 had been entered on the wrong side of a customer's account in the individual debtors ledger.

(c) A prompt payment discount of £70 had been completely omitted from the records.

(d) An invoice of £123 had been entered in the sales day book as £321.

(e) No entry had been made to record an agreement to contra an amount owed to P of £600 against an amount owed by P of £700.

(f) Bad debts of £160 had been omitted from the individual debtors accounts, but were otherwise correctly treated.

Required

Prepare journal entries to correct each of the errors described in (a) to (f) above. Accounts should be fully named, but narrative descriptions are not required.

(Total : 10 marks)

Question 26

Scimitar (ACCA 12/97)

Scimitar Limited proves the accuracy of its sales and purchases ledgers by preparing monthly control accounts. At 1 September 20X7 the following balances existed in the company's records, and the control accounts agreed.

	Debit £	*Credit* £
Sales ledger control account	188,360	2,140
Purchases ledger control account	120	89,410

The following are the totals of transactions which took place during September 20X7, as extracted from the company's records.

	£
Credit sales	101,260
Credit purchases	68,420
Sales returns	9,160
Purchases returns	4,280
Cash received from customers	91,270
Cash paid to suppliers	71,840
Cash discounts allowed	1,430
Cash discounts received	880
Bad debts written off	460
Refunds to customers	300
Contra settlements	480

At 30 September 20X7 the balances in the sales and purchases ledgers, as extracted, totalled:

	Debit £	*Credit* £
Sales ledger balances	To be ascertained	2,680
Purchases ledger balances	90	To be ascertained

An initial attempt to balance the two ledgers showed that neither of them agreed.

The differences were found to be due to the following.

(i) A credit balance of £680 had been omitted when listing the sales ledger balances.

(ii) A contra settlement of £500 had not been included in the totals of transactions prepared for the control accounts.

(iii) A new employee had mistakenly entered five copy sales invoices into the purchases day book as if they had been purchases invoices and entered the amounts to new purchases ledger accounts. The total of these invoices was £1,360.

(iv) A £20 cash refund to a customer was made out of petty cash, and has not been included in the summary of transactions given above. The £20 was entered to the sales ledger as if it had been a cash receipt from the customer, and this resulted in a £40 credit balance on the account, which was still outstanding at 30 September 20X7.

When these errors had been corrected both control accounts agreed with the ledgers.

Required

Prepare the sales ledger and purchases ledger control (total) accounts for the month of September 20X7 *after* these errors had been corrected, and hence ascertain the missing totals of the ledger balances as indicated above (debit balances in sales ledger and credit balances in purchases ledger).

(Total : 10 marks)

Question 27

Theta (ACCA 6/98)

At 31 December 20X7 the totals of the personal ledger balances of Theta Limited were as follows.

		£
Sales ledger	*debit*	384,600
	credit	2,900
Purchases ledger	*debit*	1,860
	credit	222,230

After reviewing these balances in preparing the financial statements for the year ended 31 December 20X7, a number of adjustments are necessary.

(i) A contra settlement had been agreed during the year offsetting an amount due from Zeta Limited in the sales ledger of £1,080 against the balance due to that company in the purchases ledger. No entry had been made for this contra.

(ii) The following debts due from the sales ledger customers are to be written off.

Customer	£
P	840
Q	120
R	360
S	2,090
T	180

(iii) The provision for doubtful debts, which stood at £3,060 is to be increased to £5,200.

(iv) During the year £200 cash received from Tau Limited had mistakenly been entered into the account of Vau Limited in the sales ledger.

Further information

The purchases ledger balances included £56,000 relating to a purchase in September 20X7 on extended credit terms.

The £56,000 balance is due to be cleared by payments in four equal instalments at six-monthly intervals as follows.

	£
31 March 20X8	14,000
30 September 20X8	14,000
31 March 20X9	14,000
30 September 20X9	14,000

No ledger control accounts are kept by Theta Limited.

Required

(a) Prepare journal entries to give effect to adjustments (i) to (iv). **(4 marks)**

(b) Calculate the amounts which should appear under the various headings in the company's published balance sheet as at 31 December 20X7 for debtors and creditors, assuming that there are no other items for inclusion apart from those stated above. **(6 marks)**

(Total : 10 marks)

Question 28

Computer systems

Over the past few decades, routine bookkeeping and accountancy work has been transformed by the extensive use of computers to perform that work.

Required

(a) List and briefly explain two types of error which could occur in a manual sales ledger system which could not occur in a computerised system. **(5 marks)**

(b) List and briefly explain two types of error which could occur in a manual sales ledger system which could also occur in a computerised system. **(5 marks)**

(Total : 10 marks)

Question 29

Computerised accounting systems

Explain the main advantages and disadvantages of computerised accounting systems compared with manual systems.

(Total : 10 marks)

Question 30

Andy (ACCA 6/99 adapted)

Andy had completed his financial statements for the year ending 31 March 20X9, which showed a profit of £162,416, when he realised that no bank reconciliation statement had been prepared at that date.

When checking the cash book against the bank statement and carrying out other checks he found the following:

(1) A cheque for £2,000 had been entered in the cash book but had not yet been presented.

(2) Cheques from customers totalling £5,780 entered in the cash book on 31 March 20X9 were credited by the bank on 1 April 20X9.

(3) Bank charges of £640 appear in the bank statement on 31 March 20X9 but have not been recorded by Andy.

(4) A cheque for £25,800 drawn by Andy to pay for a new item of plant had been mistakenly entered in the cash book and the plant account as £5,800. Depreciation of £580 had been charged in the profit and loss account for this plant.

(5) A cheque for £1,960 from a credit customer paid in on 26 March was dishonoured after 31 March 20X9 and Andy decided that the debt would have to be written off as the customer was now untraceable.

(6) A cheque for £4,800 in payment for some motor repairs had mistakenly been entered in the cash book as a debit and posted to the credit of motor vehicles account. Depreciation at 25% per annum (straight line) is charged on motor vehicles with a full year's charge calculated on the balance at the end of each year.

(7) The total of the payments side of the cash book had been understated by £2,000. On further investigation it was found that the debit side of the purchases account had also been understated by £2,000.

(8) Andy had instructed his bank to credit the interest of £320 on the deposit account maintained for surplus business funds to the current account. This the bank had done on 28 March. Andy had made an entry on the payments side of the cash book for this £320 and had posted it to the debit of interest payable account.

(9) Andy had mistakenly paid an account for £1,740 for repairs to his house with a cheque drawn on the business account. The entry in the cash book had been debited to repairs to premises account.

(10) Andy had also mistakenly paid £1,080 to Dave, a trade supplier, to clear his account in the purchases ledger, using a cheque drawn on Andy's personal bank account. No entries have yet been made for this transaction.

The cash book showed a debit balance of £9,780 before any correcting entries had been made. The balance in the bank statement is to be derived in your answer.

Required

(a) Prepare an adjusted cash book showing the revised balance which should appear in Andy's balance sheet at 31 March 20X9. **(3 marks)**

(b) Prepare a bank reconciliation statement as at 31 March 20X9. **(2 marks)**

(c) Draw up a statement for Andy showing the effect on his profit of the adjustments necessary to correct the errors found. **(5 marks)**

(Total : 10 marks)

Question 31

Otter (ACCA 12/99)

Otter Limited operates a computerised accounting system for its sales and purchases ledgers. The control accounts for the month of September 20X0 are in balance and incorporate the following totals:

		£
Sales ledger:		
Balances at 1 September 20X0	Debit	386,430
	Credit	190
Sales		163,194
Cash received		158,288
Discounts allowed		2,160
Sales returns inwards		590
Credit balances at 30 September 20X0		370
Purchases ledger:		
Balances at 1 September 20X0	Credit	184,740
	Debit	520
Purchases		98,192
Cash payments		103,040
Discounts received		990
Purchases returns outwards		1,370
Debit balances at 30 September 20X0		520

Although the control accounts agree with the underlying ledgers, a number of errors have been found and there are also several adjustments to be made. These errors and adjustments are detailed below.

(1) Four sales invoices totalling £1,386 have been omitted from the records.

(2) A cash refund of £350 paid to a customer, A Smith, was mistakenly treated as a payment to a supplier, A Smith Limited.

(3) A contra settlement offsetting a balance of £870 due to a supplier against the sales ledger account for the same company is to be made.

(4) Bad debts totalling £1,360 are to be written off.

(5) During the month, settlement was reached with a supplier over a disputed account. As a result, the supplier issued a credit note for £2,000 on 26 September. No entry has yet been made for this.

(6) A purchases invoice for £1,395 was keyed in as £1,359.

(7) A payment of £2,130 to a supplier, B Jones, was mistakenly entered to the account of R Jones.

(8) A debit balance of £420 existed in the purchases ledger at the end of August 20X0. The supplier concerned cannot now be traced and it has been decided to write off this balance.

Required

Prepare the sales ledger and purchases ledger control account as they should appear after allowing, where necessary, for the errors and adjustments listed.

(Total : 10 marks)

Question 32

Halberd (ACCA 12/97 adapted)

Halberd runs a fish shop. He buys supplies daily from the wholesale market paying immediately by cheque. Most of his sales are for cash, except for sales to three local restaurants, which are supplied on monthly credit terms.

Halberd keeps only partial accounting records, and he has asked for your help in preparing his profit and loss account for the year ended 30 June 20X4. In previous years, he has been assisted by a friend who is now ill and unable to continue or give any information.

Halberd has prepared an analysis of his bank transactions for the year to 30 June 20X4 and this is summarised below.

	£	£
Balance per balance sheet 30 June 20X3		3,240
Receipts		
Cash sales banked	108,600	
Receipts from credit customers (the restaurants)	28,440	
Loan received 1 January 20X4 carrying the interest at 10% per annum and repayable in 20X9	10,000	
		147,040
		150,280
Payments		
Purchase of fish for sale	81,470	
Rent and rates of shop	8,600	
Staff wages	21,400	
Drawings	20,600	
Insurance	1,400	
Van expenses	3,270	
Miscellaneous expenses	3,600	
Purchase of new shop fittings	1,570	
		141,910
Balance at 30 June 20X4		8,370

The following further information is available.

(1) Depreciation is to be provided as follows.

Refrigeration equipment:	10% on cost (straight line)
Shop fittings:	15% (reducing balance)
Van:	25% on cost (straight line)

A full year's depreciation is to be taken for the shop fittings purchased during the year.

(2) At 30 June 20X3 the following assets and liabilities existed.

		Assets £	*Liabilities* £
Stock		680	
Trade debtors		4,270	
Prepayments -	Insurance	300	
	Business rates	850	
Cash in till		100	
Amounts owing for van expenses			320
Amounts owing for miscellaneous expenses			120

(3) On 30 June 20X3, Halberd's fixed assets were:

	Cost £	*Aggregate depreciation* £	*Net book value* £
Refrigeration equipment	8,400	2,520	5,880
Shop fittings	3,720	2,090	1,630
Van	9,200	4,600	4,600

(4) At 30 June 20X4 the following assets and liabilities existed.

		Assets £	*Liabilities* £
Stock of fish for sale		810	
Trade debtors (see Note (5))		6,190	
Prepayments -	Insurance	350	
-	Business rates	1,000	
Amounts owing for miscellaneous expenses			200

(5) Halberd is worried about the amount owing by one of the restaurants. The account is three months in arrears and a provision for the full amount due of £1,860 is to be made.

(6) In addition to the drawings of £20,600 shown in the bank statement summary. Halberd always takes £300 per week (£15,600 for the year) out of the takings before banking them. He also estimates that he had taken fish costing £400 from stock for his own use during the year.

(7) Halberd had a balance of cash in his till of £150 at 30 June 20X4.

Required

Prepare Halberd's trading and profit and loss account for the year ended 30 June 20X4. Ignore VAT.

(Total : 10 marks)

Question 33

Ernie (ACCA 12/98)

Ernie is a building contractor, doing repair work for local householders. His wife keeps some accounting records but not on a double entry basis.

The assets and liabilities of the business at 30 June 20X7 were as follows.

	£
Assets	
Plant and equipment at cost	12,600
Accumulated depreciation to date	5,800
Motor van at cost	9,000
Accumulated depreciation to date	6,500
Stock of materials	14,160
Debtors	9,490
Rent of premises paid in advance to 30 September 20X7	750
Insurance paid in advance to 31 December 20X7	700
Bank balance	1,860
Cash in hand	230
Liabilities	
Creditors for supplies	3,460
Telephone bill owing	210
Electricity owing	180

His cash and bank transactions for the year from 1 July 20X7 to 30 June 20X8 are as follows.

Cash and bank summary

Receipts	*Cash* £	*Bank* £	*Payments*	*Cash* £	*Bank* £
Opening balances	230	1,860	Suppliers		83,990
Receipts from customers	52,640	150,880	Rent of premises		3,600
Loan received		10,000	Insurance (to 31.12.X8)		1,600
Proceeds of sale of vehicle held at beginning of year		3,000	Purchase of plant and equipment		8,400
Cash paid into bank		24,040	Purchase of new vehicle		12,800
Cash withdrawn from bank	48,260		Telephone		860
			Electricity		890
Closing balance		2,100	Wages of repair staff	68,200	
			Miscellaneous expenses		1,280
			Drawings by Ernie	8,000	29,800
			Refund to customer		400
			Cash paid into bank	24,040	
			Cash withdrawn from bank		48,260
			Closing balance	890	
	101,130	191,880		101,130	191,880

The following further information is available.

(1) Plant and equipment is to be depreciated at 25% per annum on the reducing balance with a full year's charge in the year of purchase.

(2) The new motor vehicle was purchased on 1 January 20X8. Ernie's depreciation policy is to charge depreciation at 25% per annum on the straight line basis, with a proportionate charge in the year of purchase, but none in the year of sale.

(3) The rent of the premises was increased by 20% from 1 October 20X7.

(4) The loan of £10,000 was obtained from Ernie's brother on 1 April 20X8. It carries interest at 10% per annum, payable on 30 September and 31 March.

(5) At 30 June 20X8, Ernie owed the following amounts.

	£
Suppliers	4,090
Telephone	240
Electricity	220
Miscellaneous expenses	490

(6) At 30 June 20X8, amounts due from customers totalled £10,860. Of this amount, Ernie considered that debts totalling £1,280 were bad and should be written off.

(7) Stock of materials at 30 June was £12,170.

(8) Ernie agreed to pay his wife £5,000 for her assistance with his office work during the year. This amount was actually paid in August 20X8.

Required

Prepare Ernie's trading and profit and loss account for the year ended 30 June 20X8.

(Total : 10 marks)

Question 34

Goshawk (ACCA 6/00)

Goshawk owns a shop selling men's and women's clothing. He purchased the shop on 1 April 20X0 paying £200,000 for a 40 year lease.

Most of Goshawk's sales are for cash, but he has a contract to supply uniforms to a small local security firm to which sales are on monthly credit terms.

At 31 March 20X1 his assets and liabilities were:

		Assets	*Liabilities*
	£	£	£
Shop		195,000	
Shop fittings cost	28,000		
Less: Accumulated depreciation	4,200		
		23,800	
Stock of goods for sale		28,500	
Trade debtors		1,380	
Prepaid insurance		800	
Cash at bank		3,600	
Loan repayable in 20X7 and carrying interest at 10% per year			100,000
Trade creditors			39,000
Miscellaneous accrued shop expenses			1,800

During the year ended 31 March 20X2, Goshawk's receipts and payments were:

	£
Receipts banked	
Sales (cash and credit customers)	299,580
(Before banking the sales revenue, cash totalling £1,300 was taken out to pay miscellaneous shop expenses)	
Payments by cheque	
Cash paid to suppliers for clothes for sale	211,830
Staff wages	25,870
Insurance	2,000
Miscellaneous shop expenses	2,180
Shop fittings purchased	8,400
Drawings by Goshawk	30,000
Refunds to cash customers for goods returned	960
Loan interest for six months to 30 September 20X1	5,000

The following further information is available.

1 Goshawk's assets and liabilities at 31 March 20X2 included the following, in addition to the shop itself and the shop fittings:

	Assets	*Liabilities*
	£	£
Stock	37,100	
Trade debtors	1,460	
Prepaid insurance	1,000	
Loan		100,000
Trade creditors		48,000
Miscellaneous accrued shop expenses		2,100

2 Appropriate amounts are to be allowed for amortisation of the lease and for depreciation of the shop fittings, consistent with previous policy, using the straight line method. A full year's depreciation is taken in the year of acquisition of fixed assets.

Required

(a) Prepare Goshawk's trading and profit and loss account for the year ended 31 March 20X2. **(7 marks)**

(b) Goshawk suspects that one of his staff has been stealing items from stock.

Prepare a statement showing the possible cost of the items stolen, using the information that all the sales are at a standard mark-up of 50% on cost, except for:

	Sales value	
	£	
Security uniform sales at a mark-up of 40% on cost	14,000	
Sales at a reduced mark-up of 25% on cost	34,000	**(3 marks)**

(Total : 10 marks)

Question 35

Zed (ACCA 6/94)

The trial balance of Zed Ltd at 1 January 20X3 contains the following items.

			£000
Bank overdraft			7
Building	-	cost	80
	-	depreciation	5
Creditors	-	trade	28
	-	operating expenses	2
16% debentures			50
Debtors			24
Land, at valuation			125
Machinery	-	cost	90
	-	depreciation	43
Ordinary shares, £1 each			100
10% preference shares, £1 each			40
Profit and loss account			34
Revaluation reserve			45
Stocks			35

Summarised transactions and events for the year to 31 December 20X3 are as follows.

(i)

	£000
Sales	920
Purchases	500
Bad debts written off	5
Contras between debtors and creditors accounts	8
Operating expenses paid	360

(ii) 30,000 £1 ordinary shares were issued at £2.00 per share on 1 January 20X3; this transaction was not reflected in the trial balance above.

(iii) Debenture interest and the preference dividend for the year were all paid on 31 December. An ordinary dividend of 20p per share was paid on 31 December.

(iv) The land is revalued at 31 December 20X3 to £130,000. The machinery is to be depreciated at 10% on cost and the buildings are to be depreciated on the straight line basis over 80 years.

(v) The following additional information is available at 31 December 20X3.

	£000
Additional operating expenses owing are	10
Closing stock is	40
Closing debtors are	35
Closing trade creditors are	25

Required

Prepare the balance sheet at 31 December 20X3. This statement does not need to comply with Companies Act disclosure requirements, but should be presented in a format which is generally accepted and which presents the information helpful to the reader. Submit all workings. Ignore taxation.

(Total : 10 marks)

Question 36

Provision

Define and explain the difference between a provision and a reserve, giving one example of each (other than a provision for doubtful debts).

(Total : 10 marks)

Question 37

Grace

You are given the following trial balance of Grace Ltd as at 31 December 20X7, as prepared by the firm's bookkeeper. All figures are in £000.

	Dr *£000*	*Cr* *£000*
Share capital (200,000 50p shares)		100
Share premium		50
Profit and loss balance 1 January 20X7		100
Debentures (10% interest pa) issued in 20X4		100
Stock	200	
Motor vehicles	100	
Motor vehicles depreciation 1 January 20X7		60
Machinery	120	

Machinery depreciation 1 January 20X7		50
Buildings at cost 1 January 20X7	230	
Sales		750
Purchases	350	
Discounts	2	
Returns	2	
Carriage	2	
General expenses	200	
Advertising	10	
Creditors		200
Debtors	200	
Provision for doubtful debts		6
Debenture interest	5	
Bank balance		5
	1,421	1,421

You are also given the following information.

(1) The bookkeeper, in an attempt at simplification, has posted both discounts received and discounts allowed to the discounts account. He has also posted both returns inwards and returns outwards to the returns account, and both carriage inwards and carriage outwards to the carriage account.

Discounts received were actually	£1,000
Returns outwards were actually	£1,000
Carriage outwards were actually	£1,000

(2) The following items are already included in general expenses.

(i) Rates for the 12 months to 31 March 20X8, £4,000.

(ii) Insurance for the 12 months to 31 December 20X8, £2,000. Half of this amount relates to the managing director's private yacht.

(3) Your own charges of £1,000 for accountancy services need to be included.

(4) A debtor of £20,000 has gone bankrupt. The provision for doubtful debts is required to be 5% of debtors.

(5) A dividend of 5p per share is proposed.

(6) Closing stock is £180,000.

(7) Depreciation of £20,000 is to be provided on the motor vehicles and of £10,000 on the machinery.

Required

Prepare a profit and loss account for Grace Ltd for the year (for internal purposes).

(Total : 10 marks)

Question 38

Arbalest (ACCA 12/97)

The summarised balance sheet of Arbalest Limited at 30 September 20X6 was as follows.

	Cost £000	Aggregate depreciation £000	Net book value £000
Fixed assets			
Land	2,000	Nil	2,000
Buildings	1,500	450	1,050
Plant and machinery	2,800	1,000	1,800
	6,300	1,450	4,850
Current assets		3,180	
Current liabilities		2,070	1,110
			5,960
Capital and reserves			
Called-up share capital:			
3,000,000 ordinary shares of 50p each			1,500
Share premium account			400
Profit and loss account			4,060
			5,960

During the year ended 30 September 20X7 the company had the following transactions.

1 *1 November 20X6*

A rights issue of one share for every three held at a price of £1.50 per share. All the rights issue shares were taken up.

2 *1 December 20X6*

Sale for £70,000 of plant and machinery which had cost £1,000,000 and had a book value of £200,000.

3 *1 March 20X7*

A bonus (capitalisation) issue of one share for every one held at that date using the share premium account as far as possible for the purpose.

4 *1 June 20X7*

Purchased a new factory block for £3,000,000 (including land £600,000).

5 *1 July 20X7*

Purchased plant and machinery for £1,600,000.

6 *30 September 20X7*

The company decided to revalue the freehold land held at 30 September 20X6 from £2,000,000 to £2,500,000.

The company depreciation policies are as follows.

Land	No depreciation
Buildings	2% per annum on cost, straight-line basis
Plant and machinery	10% per annum on cost, straight-line basis

Proportionate depreciation is provided in the year of purchase of an asset, with none in the year of disposal. The retained profit for the year was £370,000.

Required

Prepare the notes required for the company's balance sheet for publication at 30 September 20X7 detailing:

(a) movements on reserves.
(b) movements on fixed assets.

Ledger accounts for the transactions are *not* required.

(Total : 10 marks)

Question 39

Koppa Ltd (ACCA 6/98)

The following balances existed in the accounting records of Koppa Limited at 31 December 20X7.

		£000
Development costs capitalised, 1 January 20X7		180
Freehold land as revalued 31 December 20X7		2,200
Buildings	cost	900
	aggregate depreciation at 1 January 20X7	100
Office equipment	cost	260
	aggregate depreciation at 1 January 20X7	60
Motor vehicles	cost	200
	aggregate depreciation at 1 January 20X7	90
Trade debtors		1,360
Cash at bank		90
Trade creditors		820
12% debentures (issued 20X0 and redeemable 20X7)		1,000
Called up share capital – ordinary shares of 50p each		1,000
Share premium account		500
Revaluation reserve		200
Profit and loss account 1 January 20X7		1,272
Sales		8,650
Purchases		5,010
Research and development expenditure for the year		162
Stock 1 January 20X7		990
Distribution costs		460
Administrative expenses		1,560
Debenture interest		120
Interim dividend paid		200

In preparing the company's financial statements at 31 December 20X7 the following further information is relevant.

(1) Stock at 31 December 20X7 was £880,000.

(2) Depreciation is to be provided for as follows.

Land	Nil
Buildings	2% per annum on cost
Office equipment	20% per annum, reducing balance basis
Motor vehicles	25% per annum on cost

(3) The £180,000 total for development costs as at 1 January 20X7 relates to two projects.

	£000
Project 836: completed project: (balance being amortised: over the period expected to benefit from it. Amount to be amortised in 20X7 £20,000)	82
Project 910: in progress	98
	180

(4) The research and development expenditure for the year is made up of the following.

	£000
Research expenditure	103
Development costs on Project 910 which continues to satisfy the requirements in SSAP 13 for capitalisation	59
	162

(5) The freehold land had originally cost £2,000,000 and was revalued on 31 December 20X7.

(6) Prepayments and accruals at 31 December 20X7 were as follows.

	Prepayments *£000*	*Accruals* *£000*
Administrative expenses	40	11
Sundry distribution costs		4

(7) The share premium account balance arose as a result of the issue during 20X7 of 1,000,000 50p ordinary shares at £1.00 each. All share qualify for the proposed final dividend to be provided for (see note below).

(8) A final dividend of 20p per share is proposed.

Required

Prepare the company's balance sheet as at 31 December 20X7, in a form suitable for publication as far as the information provided permits. The note detailing reserve movements for the year should be given, but no other notes are required. Ignore taxation.

(Total : 10 marks)

Question 40

Topaz (ACCA 6/97)

Topaz Limited makes up its accounts regularly to 31 December each year. The company has operated for some years with four divisions A, B, C and D, but on 30 June 20X6 Division B was sold for £8m, realising a profit of £2.5m. During 20X6 there was a fundamental reorganisation of Division C, the costs of which were £1.8m.

The trial balance of the company at 31 December 20X6 included the following balances.

	Division B		*Divisions A, C and D combined*	
	Dr	*Cr*	*Dr*	*Cr*
	£m	*£m*	*£m*	*£m*
Sales		13		68
Cost of sales	8		41	
Distribution costs (including a bad debt of £1.9m – Division D)	1		6	
Administrative expenses	2		4	
Profit on sale of Division B		2.5		
Reorganisation costs, Division C			1.8	
Interest on £10m 10% debenture stock issued in 20X0			1	
Taxation			4.8	
Interim dividend paid			2	
Revaluation reserve				10

The balance on the revaluation reserve relates to the company's freehold property and arose as follows.

	£m
Balance at 1 January 20X6	6
Revaluation during 20X6	4
Balance at 31 December 20X6 per trial balance	10

The final proposed dividend was £4m.

Required

(a) Prepare the profit and loss account of Topaz Limited for the year ended 31 December 20X6, complying as far as possible with the provisions of the Companies Act 1985 and FRS 3 *Reporting Financial Performance.*

(b) Prepare the statement of total recognised gains and losses for the year as required by FRS 3.

(Total : 10 marks)

Question 41

FRS 3 (ACCA 12/98)

(a) FRS 3 *Reporting Financial Performance* includes requirements governing the treatment of certain items in the published profit and loss account.

Required

Explain how FRS 3 requires discontinued operations and acquisitions to be dealt with in the profit and loss account. What are the advantages of these requirements to users of financial statements? **(7 marks)**

(b) FRS 3 also requires the presentation of a statement of recognised gains and losses. State three items which could appear in this statement. **(3 marks)**

(Total : 10 marks)

Question 42

Leonardo (ACCA 12/98)

The trial balance of Leonardo Limited at 30 September 20X8 included the following items.

	Dr	*Cr*
	£000	*£000*
Sales		6,840
Opening stock	1,200	
Purchases	3,670	
Distribution costs	880	
Administrative expenses	590	
Interest payable	300	
Costs of a fundamental reorganisation of company's operations	560	
Profit on sale of head office building (the company plans to move its central administration into a rented building)		1,200
Provision for doubtful debts 1 October 20X7		150

In preparing the company's profit and loss account the following further information is to be taken into account.

(i) A stock count was taken on 27 September 20X8 (all valued at cost) and amounted to £950,000. Between that date and the close of business on 30 September 20X8, goods costing £68,000 were sold, and there were no further receipts of goods. These sales are included in the sales total of £6,840,000.

(ii) During the year a debt of £400,000 proved to be irrecoverable and is to be written off. The provision for doubtful debts is to be increased to £200,000.

(iii) The tax charge on the profit from ordinary activities was £300,000.

Required

Prepare the company's profit and loss account for the year ended 30 September 20X8 for publication and complying, so far as the information permits, with the requirements of FRS 3.

Note. Marks are awarded for layout and style as well as for the correct calculation of the figures required for the answer.

(Total : 10 marks)

Question 43

Atok (ACCA 12/99)

Atok Limited compiles its financial statements to 30 June annually. At 30 June 20X1, the company's trial balance was as follows:

		£000	£000
Sales revenue			14,800
Purchases		8,280	
Stock at 1 July 20X0		1,390	
Distribution costs		1,080	
Administrative expenses		1,460	
Land at valuation		10,500	
Buildings:	cost	8,000	
	accumulated depreciation at 1 July 20X0		2,130
Plant and equipment:	cost	12,800	
	accumulated depreciation at 1 July 20X0		2,480
Trade debtors and creditors		4,120	2,240
Cash at bank		160	
Ordinary shares of 50p each:	as at 1 July 20X0		10,000
	issued during year		4,000
Share premium account:	as at 1 July 20X0		2,000
	arising on shares issued during year		2,000
Revaluation reserve as at 1 July 20X0			3,000
Profit and loss account			3,140
10% debentures (redeemable 20X0) (issued 1 April 20X1 with interest payable 31 March and 30 Sept each year)			2,000
		47,790	47,790

The following matters remain to be adjusted for in preparing the financial statements for the year ended 30 June 20X1.

(1) Stock at 30 June 20X1 amounted to £1,560,000 at cost. A review of stock items revealed the need for some adjustments for two stock lines:

(i) items which had cost £80,000 and which would normally sell for £120,000 were found to have deteriorated. Remedial work costing £20,000 would be needed to enable the items to be sold for £90,000.

(ii) some items sent to customers on sale or return terms had been omitted from stock and included as sales in June 20X1. The cost of these items was £16,000 and they were included in sales at £24,000. In July 20X1, the items were returned in good condition by the customers.

(2) Depreciation is to be provided as follows:

Buildings	2% per year on cost
Plant and equipment	20% per year on cost

80% of the depreciation is to be charged in cost of sales, and 10% each in distribution costs and administrative expenses.

(3) The land is to be revalued to £12,000,000. No change was required to the value of the buildings.

(4) Accruals and prepayments were:

	Accruals £000	*Prepayments* £000
Distribution costs	190	120
Administrative expenses	70	60

(5) A dividend of 2½ pence per share is proposed. All shares in issue at 30 June 20X1 qualify for this dividend.

Required

(a) Prepare the company's profit and loss account for the year ended 30 June 20X1 for publication, complying as far as possible with the provisions of the Companies Acts and accounting standards. **(7 marks)**

(b) Prepare a statement detailing all reserve movements during the year. Other notes to the financial statements are *not* required. **(3 marks)**

(Total : 10 marks)

Question 44

Lark (ACCA 6/00)

An extract from the trial balance of Lark Limited for the year ended 31 March 20X0 is given below.

	£000	*£000*
Sales		20,000
Cost of sales	12,300	
Distribution costs	2,100	
Administrative expenses	3,600	
Interest receivable		1,200
Interest payable	800	

The taxation charge for the year is estimated to be £480,000.

During the year the company sold trading Division B.

The extracts from the company's trial balance shown above include the following items for Division B.

	£000	£000
Sales		6,000
Cost of sales	4,800	
Distribution costs	840	
Administrative expenses (excluding the loss on disposal £400,000 shown below)	700	

The total of £3,600,000 for administrative expenses is currently made up as follows.

	£000
General administrative expenses	
Continuing activities	1,930
Discontinued activities as shown above	700
Bad debt arising from the insolvency of a major customer in continuing activities	360
Cost of a fundamental reorganisation of continuing activities	210
Loss on disposal of trading Division B	400
	3,600

Required

Prepare the company's profit and loss account for publication for the year ended 31 March 20X0 in accordance with the Companies Act 1985 and FRS 3 *Reporting Financial Performance*. Include any note you consider necessary.

(Total : 10 marks)

Question 45

Notes or statements

FRS 3 requires companies to produce several other statements or notes in addition to the profit and loss account and balance sheet. Name and briefly describe the contents of three of these statements or notes.

(Total : 10 marks)

Question 46

Moorfoot (ACCA 12/00)

Moorfoot Limited operates a chain of wholesale grocery outlets. Its trial balance at 30 June 20X1 was as follows.

	£000	£000
Sales revenue		13,600
Purchases	8,100	
Stock 1 July 20X0	1,530	
Distribution costs	1,460	
Administrative expenses	1,590	
Interest on debentures	50	
Interim dividend paid	360	
Freehold land at cost	1,510	
Buildings		
- Cost	8,300	
- Accumulated depreciation at 30 June 20X0		1,020
Warehouse and office equipment		
- Cost	1,800	
- Accumulated depreciation at 30 June 20X0		290
Motor vehicles		
- Cost	1,680	
- Accumulated depreciation at 30 June 20X0		620
Trade debtors	810	
Provision for doubtful debts		18
Cash at bank	140	
Trade creditors		820
10% debentures (issued 20W6 and to be redeemed 20X1)		1,000
Called up share capital – ordinary shares of 25p each		1,200
Share premium account		2,470
Profit and loss account 30 June 20X0		6,292
	27,330	27,330

The following additional information is available.

(1) Closing stock was £1,660,000.

(2) Trade debts totalling £6,000 are to be written off and the provision for doubtful debts increased to £30,000. It is the company's practice to include the charge for bad and doubtful debts in administrative expenses in the profit and loss account.

(3) Accruals and prepayments:

	Prepayments £000	*Accruals* £000
Distribution costs	60	120
Administrative expenses	70	190
Interest on debentures		50

(4) In early July 20X1 the company received invoices for credit purchases totalling £18,000 for goods delivered before 30 June. These invoices have not been included in the purchases ledger at 30 June 20X1.

It was also found that credit sales invoices totalling £7,000 for goods delivered to customers before 30 June 20X1 had mistakenly been dated in July 20X1 and thus excluded from sales for the year and from debtors at the year end.

The goods received had been included in the year end stock figure given at (1) above, and the goods sold had been excluded from it. No adjustment to the stock figure is therefore required.

(5) Depreciation should be provided as follows:

Land	Nil
Buildings	2% per year on cost
Warehouse and office equipment	15% per year on cost
Motor vehicles	25% per year on cost

All depreciation is to be divided equally between distribution costs and administrative expenses.

(6) A final dividend of 10p per share is proposed.

Required

Prepare the company's profit and loss account for the year ended 30 June 20X1, complying as far as possible with the requirements of the Companies Act 1985. Ignore taxation. Notes to the financial statements are not required.

(Total : 10 marks)

Question 47

GAAP and FRS 3

(a) Neither the share premium account nor the revaluation reserve is distributable by way of dividend. Explain why it would be contrary to generally accepted accounting principles if these balances were to be distributable as dividend.

(4 marks)

(b) Explain why the changes to the profit and loss account introduced by FRS 3 improve the quality of information available to users of the financial statements. **(6 marks)**

(Total : 10 marks)

Question 48

Prince plc

On 1 January 20X4 Prince plc acquired 100% of the share capital of Madonna Ltd, paying £60,000 for its investment.

The balance sheets of the two companies are as follows at 31 December 20X4:

		Prince	*Madonna*
		£	£
Fixed assets:	Tangible	100,000	40,000
	Investments	60,000	–
		160,000	40,000
Current assets		90,000	86,000
Creditors: Amounts falling due within one year		(50,000)	(41,000)
Net current assets		40,000	45,000
Total assets less current liabilities		200,000	85,000
Creditors: Amounts falling due after more than one year		(18,000)	(30,000)
		182,000	55,000
Share capital		60,000	50,000
Profit and loss account		122,000	5,000
		182,000	55,000

Profit for the year:

	£
Prince plc	3,000
Madonna Ltd	1,000

Goodwill arising on acquisition is amortised through the profit and loss account over three years from the date of acquisition.

Required

Show how the consolidated balance sheet would look at 31 December 20X4.

Question 49

Heavy plc

As on 31 March 20X1 the draft balance sheets of Heavy plc and its subsidiary, Side Ltd showed the following positions:

	Heavy plc		Side Ltd	
	£	£	£	£
Fixed assets (tangible)		180,000		40,000
Investment in Side Ltd		49,200		-
		229,200		40,000
Current assets				
Stock	40,000		32,000	
Cash at bank and in hand	-		13,500	
	40,000		45,500	
Creditors: Amounts falling due within one year				
Bank overdraft	14,000		-	
Trade creditors	41,000		17,000	
	55,000		17,000	
Net current (liabilities)/assets		(15,000)		28,500
Total assets less current liabilities		214,200		68,500
Creditors: Amounts falling due after more than one year				
Debenture loan		(50,000)		-
		164,200		68,500
Financed by:				
Share capital – £1 ordinary shares		100,000		10,000
Share premium account		20,000		10,000
Profit and loss account		44,200		48,500
		164,200		68,500

You are given the following additional information:

(1) It has been decided that Heavy plc should declare a dividend of 10 pence per share for the year ended 31 March 20X1.

(2) Heavy plc acquired 80% of the issued share capital of Side Ltd on 1 April 20X0. Side Ltd made a profit available for distribution for the year of £10,500.

(3) It is group accounting policy to amortise any goodwill on acquisition through the profit and loss account over five years.

Required

Prepare the consolidated balance sheet of Heavy plc as on 31 March 20X1, together with your consolidation schedules.

Question 50

Roxy

The financial statements of Roxy Ltd at 30 June were as follows.

BALANCE SHEETS AT 30 JUNE

	20X8		*20X7*	
	£	£	£	£
Tangible fixed assets				
Building				
Cost	22,000		12,000	
Depreciation	(4,000)		(1,000)	
		18,000		11,000
Plant and machinery				
Cost	5,000		5,000	
Depreciation	(2,250)		(2,000)	
		2,750		3,000
		20,750		14,000
Current assets				
Stock	16,000		11,000	
Debtors	9,950		2,700	
Bank and cash	-		1,300	
	25,950		15,000	

Creditors: amounts falling due within one year				
Bank overdraft	11,000		-	
Trade creditors	8,000		11,000	
Tax creditor	1,800		1,000	
Accrual for interest	700		200	
	21,500		12,200	
Net current assets		4,450		2,800
		25,200		16,800
Creditors: amounts falling due after more than one year				
Loan		(6,000)		(10,000)
		19,200		6,800
Capital and reserves				
Ordinary share capital		3,000		3,000
Profit and loss account		16,200		3,800
		19,200		6,800

Profit and loss account (extracts)

	20X8 £	*20X7* £
Operating profit	15,400	5,900
Interest charge	(1,000)	(1,400)
Profit before tax	14,400	4,500
Taxation	(2,000)	(1,500)
Retained profit for the year	12,400	3,000

Machinery with a net book value of £250 was sold at the beginning of 20X8 for £350. This machinery had originally cost £1,000.

No dividends have been paid in recent years.

Required

Prepare a cash flow statement for the year ended 30 June 20X8, including a reconciliation of operating profit to operating cash flow.

(Total : 10 marks)

Question 51

Rapier (ACCA 12/97)

The balance sheets of Rapier Limited at 30 September 20X6 and 30 September 20X7 are given below.

BALANCE SHEETS AT 30 SEPTEMBER

	20X6		*20X7*	
	£000	*£000*	*£000*	*£000*
Fixed assets (see Note 1)				
Cost	600		730	
Aggregate depreciation	220	380	240	490
Current assets				
Stock	81		90	
Debtors	90		86	
Cash	4		7	
	175		183	
Current liabilities				
Trade creditors	48		50	
Bank overdraft	13		18	
Proposed dividends	18		22	
	79		90	
Net current assets		96		93
		476		583
10% debentures (see Note 2)		(100)		(50)
		376		533
Capital and reserves				
Ordinary shares of £1 each		150		200
Share premium account		50		80
Revaluation reserve		-		50
Profit and loss account		176		203
		376		533

Notes

1 *Fixed assets*

During the year fixed assets which had cost £100,000, and which had a book value at 30 September 20X6 of £20,000, were sold for £25,000.

2 *Debentures*

Interest is due half-yearly on 31 March and 30 September and was paid on the due dates. £50,000 of the 10% debentures were repaid on 30 September 20X7.

3 *Share capital*

The increase in share capital took place on 1 January 20X7.

4 An interim dividend of 5p per share was paid on 6 May 20X7 to holders of all shares in issue at that date.

5 Taxation has not been allowed for and is to be ignored in your answer.

Required

Prepare a cash flow statement for the year ended 30 September 20X7 using the indirect method.

Your answer should comply as far as possible with the requirements of FRS 1 as revised and should include the reconciliation of operating profit to net cash flow from operating activities.

The note reconciling net cash flow with movement in net debt is *not* required.

(Total : 10 marks)

Question 52

Weasel (ACCA 12/99)

The balance sheets of Weasel plc at 31 August 20X0 and 20X1 are given below.

	Notes	*Year ended 31 August*			
		20X0		*20X1*	
		£000	*£000*	*£000*	*£000*
Fixed assets	1		6,400		8,500
Current assets					
Stock		1,200		1,400	
Debtors		1,500		1,400	
Cash at bank		200		300	
		2,900		3,100	
Creditors: amounts falling due within one year					
Trade creditors		(800)		(700)	
Taxation		(400)		(500)	
Bank overdraft		(360)		(200)	
Net current assets			1,340		1,700
Total assets less current liabilities			7,740		10,200
Creditors: amounts falling due after more than one year					
10% debentures 20X7	3		(1,000)		(1,500)
			6,740		8,700

Capital and reserves		
Called up share capital	2,000	2,200
Share premium account	2,340	2,540
Revaluation reserve	-	1,000
Profit and loss account	2,400	2,960
	6,740	8,700

Notes

(1) Movements in fixed assets:

	Land	Buildings	Plant and equipment	Total
	£000	£000	£000	£000
Cost or valuation				
At 1 September 20X0	2,000	3,000	3,400	8,400
Additions			2,500	2,500
Disposals			(1,000)	(1,000)
Revaluation	1,000			1,000
At 31 August 20X1	3,000	3,000	4,900	10,900
Accumulated depreciation				
At 1 September 20X0		400	1,600	2,000
Provision for year		60	1,140	1,200
Disposals			(800)	(800)
At 31 August 20X1		460	1,940	2,400
Net book amounts				
At 31 August 20X1	3,000	2,540	2,960	8,500
At 1 September 20X0	2,000	2,600	1,800	6,400

(2) Dividends paid during the year amounted to £500,000.

(3) Issue of debentures – a further £500,000 of 10% debentures was issued at par on 1 September 20X0. Interest on all debentures is paid on 28 February and 31 August each year.

(4) Plant sold during the year realised £250,000.

(5) The tax charge for the year in the profit and loss account was £500,000.

Required

Prepare a cash flow statement for Weasel plc for the year ended 31 August 20X1, complying as far as possible with FRS 1 *Cash Flow Statements*, using the indirect method.

The note reconciling operating profit to operating cash flows must be shown, but *no* other notes are required.

(Total : 10 marks)

Question 53

Fintry (ACCA 12/00)

The balance sheets of Fintry Limited at 30 September 20X0 and 30 September 20X1 are as follows.

	Notes	30 September			
		20X0		20X1	
		£000	£000	£000	£000
Fixed assets					
Cost/revaluation		2,740		4,995	
Accumulated depreciation	1	700		1,000	
			2,040		3,995
Current assets					
Stock		380		490	
Debtors		410		380	
Cash		10		15	
		800		885	
Current liabilities					
Creditors		200		250	
Bank overdraft		80		70	
Proposed dividend	2	60		80	
		340		400	
Net current assets			460		485
			2,500		4,480
12% debentures	3		(500)		(1,000)
			2,000		3,480
Capital and reserves					
Ordinary shares of 50p each	5		1,000		1,500
Share premium account			600		800
Revaluation reserve			-		400
Profit and loss account			400		780
			2,000		3,480

Notes

1 *Fixed assets*

During the year, land carried in the accounts at cost £800,000 was revalued to £1,200,000. No depreciation had been provided on this land.

Also, fixed assets which had cost £200,000 were sold for £55,000. Their book value at the time of sale was £40,000.

2 *Dividends*

An interim dividend of 2p per share was paid on 10 May 20X1.

3 *Debentures*

£500,000 of debentures were issued on 1 October 20X0.

4 *Bank overdraft interest*

Interest on the bank overdraft for the year was £8,000.

5 *Share issue*

1,000,000 ordinary shares were issued on 1 July 20X1 at a price of 70p per share.

Required

Prepare a cash flow statement for the year ended 30 September 20X1, using the indirect method and complying as far as possible with FRS 1 *Cash Flow Statements*.

Your answer should include the reconciliation of operating profit to net cash flow but the note reconciling net cash flow with movement in net debt is *not* required. Ignore taxation.

(Total : 10 marks)

Question 54

Emerald (ACCA 6/97)

Emerald Limited and Garnet Limited are two companies engaged in manufacturing electrical appliances. Both operate from rented premises. Their financial statements at 31 March 20X7 were as follows.

PROFIT AND LOSS ACCOUNT FOR THE YEAR ENDED 31 MARCH 20X7

	Emerald		*Garnet*	
	£000	*£000*	*£000*	*£000*
Sales		1,075		756
Materials	360		280	
Manufacturing wages	130		140	
Depreciation of plant	125		74	
Other manufacturing costs	100		80	
Cost of sales		(715)		(574)
Gross profit		360		182
Sundry expenses		(125)		(85)
Operating profit		235		87
Interest on debentures		(10)		(30)
Net profit before tax		225		57
Taxation		(50)		(15)
Net profit after tax		175		42
Proposed dividend		(100)		(40)
Retained profit		75		2

BALANCE SHEETS AS AT 31 MARCH 20X7

	Emerald		Garnet	
	£000	£000	£000	£000
Tangible fixed assets				
Plant and machinery at cost	1,250		1,480	
Aggregate depreciation	(450)		(1,160)	
		800		320
Office equipment at cost	65		180	
Aggregate depreciation	(20)		(82)	
		45		98
Motor vehicles at cost	60		50	
Aggregate depreciation	(20)		(20)	
		40		30
		885		448
Current assets				
Stock	210		170	
Trade debtors	400		300	
Sundry debtors	50		40	
Cash at bank	20			
	680		510	
Current liabilities				
Trade creditors	100		140	
Sundry creditors (including taxation)	80		60	
Overdraft at bank	100		280	
Proposed dividend	100		40	
	380		520	
Net current assets (liabilities)		300		(10)
		1,185		438
10% debentures		(100)		(300)
		1,085		138
Capital and reserves				
Called up share capital		600		100
Profit and loss account		485		38
		1,085		138

Required

(a) Calculate the following ratios for both companies.

(i) Current ratio
(ii) Quick ratio/acid test
(iii) Return on capital employed (ROCE)
(iv) Return on owners' equity (before taxation)
(v) Gross profit percentage on sales
(vi) Operating profit percentage on sales **(5 marks)**

(b) Comment briefly on the relative profitability and liquidity of the two companies. **(5 marks)**

(Total : 10 marks)

Question 55

Beta (ACCA 12/98)

Beta Limited is reviewing the financial statements of two companies, Zeta Limited and Omega Limited.

The companies trade as wholesalers, selling electrical goods to retailers on credit.

Their most recent financial statements are below.

BALANCE SHEETS AS AT 31 MARCH 20X8

	Zeta Limited		*Omega Limited*	
	£000	*£000*	*£000*	*£000*
Fixed assets				
Tangible assets				
Warehouse and office buildings	1,200		5,000	
Equipment and vehicles	600		1,000	
		1,800		6,000
Current assets				
Stock	400		800	
Trade debtors	800		900	
Sundry debtors	150		80	
Cash at bank	-		100	
	1,350		1,880	
Current liabilities				
Trade creditors	800		800	
Sundry creditors	80		100	
Overdraft	200		-	
Taxation	120		90	
	1,200		990	

	Zeta Limited	Omega Limited
Net current assets	150	890
	1,950	6,890
Long-term loan (interest 10% per annum)	-	(4,000)
	1,950	2,890
Capital and reserves		
Share capital	1,000	1,600
Revaluation reserve	-	500
Profit and loss account	950	790
	1,950	2,890

PROFIT AND LOSS ACCOUNTS FOR THE YEAR ENDED 31 MARCH 20X8

	Zeta Limited		*Omega Limited*	
	£000	*£000*	*£000*	*£000*
Sales		4,000		6,000
Cost of sales				
Opening stock	200		800	
Purchases	3,200		4,800	
	3,400		5,600	
Less closing stock	400		800	
		3,000		4,800
Gross profit		1,000		1,200
Expenses				
Distribution costs	200		150	
Administrative expenses	290		250	
Interest paid	10		400	
		500		800
Profit before tax		500		400
Taxation		120		90
Net profit for the period		380		310

Required

(a) Calculate for each company a total of four ratios which will assist in measuring the two aspects of liquidity and management of the elements of working capital. Show all workings. **(4 marks)**

(b) Based on the ratios you have calculated in (a), compare the two companies as regards their liquidity and working capital managements. **(4 marks)**

(c) Omega Limited is much more highly geared than Zeta Limited. What are the implications of this for the two companies? **(2 marks)**

(Total : 10 marks)

Question 56

Hawk (ACCA 12/00)

The directors of Hawk Limited wish to compare the company's most recent financial statements with those of the previous year as regards profitability and liquidity. The company's financial statements are given below.

HAWK LIMITED – PROFIT AND LOSS ACCOUNTS

	Year ended	
	31 March 20X0	*31 March 20X1*
	£000	*£000*
Sales revenue (80% on credit and 20% cash)	1,800	2,500
Cost of sales (see note below)	(1,200)	(1,800)
Gross profit	600	700
Distribution costs	(160)	(250)
Administrative expenses	(200)	(200)
Operating profit	240	250
Interest payable	(50)	(50)
Profit before tax	190	200
Taxation	(44)	(46)
Retained profit	146	154

Note. Cost of sales figures are made up as follows:

	Year ended	
	31 March 20X0	*31 March 20X1*
	£000	*£000*
Opening stock	180	200
Purchases (all on credit)	1,220	1,960
	1,400	2,160
Less closing stock	(200)	(360)
Cost of sales	1,200	1,800

	Balance sheets as at			
	31 March 20X0		*31 March 20X1*	
	£000	*£000*	*£000*	*£000*
Fixed assets – cost	3,100		3,674	
Less accumulated depreciation	1,214		1,422	
		1,886		2,252

Current assets				
Stock	200		360	
Debtors – trade	400		750	
Cash at bank	100		120	
	700		1,230	
Less current liabilities				
Creditors – trade	(210)		(380)	
Creditors – sundry	(260)		(430)	
Taxation	(48)		(50)	
	(518)		(860)	
Net current assets		182		370
Total assets less current liabilities		2,068		2,622
10% debentures		500		500
		1,568		2,122
Capital and reserves				
Issued ordinary share capital	1,000		1,200	
Share premium account	400		600	
Profit and loss account	168		322	
		1,568		2,122
		1,568		2,122

Note. The additional share capital was issued on 1 April 20X0.

Required

(a) Calculate, for each of the two years, five accounting ratios which should assist the directors in their comparison, using closing figures for balance sheet items needed. **(5 marks)**

(b) Suggest possible reasons for the changes in the ratios between the two years. **(5 marks)**

(Total : 10 marks)

Question 57

Goodwill

(a) Explain how the goodwill of a business is created. **(2 marks)**

(b) Distinguish between purchased goodwill and inherent goodwill. **(2 marks)**

(c) Explain the recommended accounting treatment for each type of goodwill and the reasons for that treatment. **(6 marks)**

(Total : 10 marks)

Question 58

Standards (ACCA 6/97)

The directors of a company are reviewing the company's most recent draft financial statements and the following points have been raised for discussion.

(a) *Post balance sheet events*

Shortly after the balance sheet date a major debtor of the company went into liquidation because of heavy trading losses and it is expected that little or nothing will be recoverable for the debt.

In the financial statements the debt has been written off, but one of the directors has pointed out that, as a post balance sheet event, the debt should not in fact be written off but disclosure should be made by note to this year's financial statements, and the debt written off next year. **(5 marks)**

(b) *Contingency*

An ex-director of the company has commenced an action against the company claiming substantial damages for wrongful dismissal. The company's solicitors have advised that the ex-director is unlikely to succeed with his claim. The solicitors' estimates of the company's potential liabilities are as follows.

	£
Legal costs (to be incurred whether the claim is successful or not)	50,000
Settlement of claim if successful	500,000
	550,000

At present, there is no provision or note for this contingency. **(5 marks)**

Required

State with reasons whether you consider the accounting treatments in the draft financial statements, as described above, are acceptable. Include in your answer, where appropriate, an explanation of the relevant provisions of accounting standards (SSAPs and FRSs).

(Total : 10 marks)

Question 59

Rubens (ACCA 12/98)

Rubens plc is a company in the pharmaceuticals industry which spends heavily on research and development each year. The company's policy is to capitalise development expenditure meeting the conditions in SSAP 13 *Research and Development* and to amortise it over five years on the straight line basis beginning when sales revenue is first generated from the developed product. Amortisation is apportioned on a time basis in the first year of amortisation.

The company's finance director has asked you to compute the amounts for research and development to be included in the financial statements for the year ended 30 September 20X8 in accordance with the company's accounting policy. The company's profit is expected to be about £8 million.

The company's ledger accounts for development expenditure and research expenditure, before amortisation and other adjustments for the year ended 30 September 20X8, showed the following details.

Development expenditure

Profit	*Balance at 30 September 20X7 £000*	*Expenditure year ended 30 September 20X8 £000*	*Balance at 30 September 20X8 £000*
A	600		
B	2,400		
C	3,600	400	4,000
D	1,200	300	1,500
E		800	800
F		400	400

Notes on the projects

Project A was completed in 20X5 at a total cost of £1,000,000 and is being amortised in accordance with the company's policy.

Project B was completed in June 20X7. Sales revenue began on 1 November 20X7.

Project C is not yet complete and development is proceeding. It continues to meet the criteria for capitalisation in SSAP 13.

Project D was abandoned during the year ended 30 September 20X8 when a competitor launched a superior product.

Project E is a new development project commenced in 20X7/X8. It meets the criteria for capitalisation in SSAP 13.

Project F was commenced and completed during 20X7/X8. Sales revenue is expected to begin in 20X9.

Research expenditure

The balance on the research expenditure account was £1,800,000, representing payments made during the year ended 30 September 20X8.

Required

(a) State the criteria which must be met under SSAP 13 *Research and Development* if development expenditure is to be capitalised. **(5 marks)**

(b) Compute the amounts to be included in the profit and loss account for research and development expenditure and in the balance sheet for deferred expenditure, and state the heading under which they should be included or disclosed. **(5 marks)**

(Total : 10 marks)

Question 60

Ochil (ACCA 12/00)

The draft financial statements of Ochil Limited for the year ended 31 March 20X1 are currently under consideration by the directors. The profit for the year is shown as £350,000.

Since 31 March 20X1 the following events have occurred, but have not been reflected in any way in the draft financial statements to that date:

(1) A substantial quantity of slow-moving stock was sold for £160,000. The stock had cost £300,000 and had been valued for the accounts at 31 March at its estimated net realisable value of £200,000.

(2) A trade debtor paid the amount owing of £65,000 in full. At 31 March there were doubts as to whether it would be paid and a specific provision for the full amount had been made in the accounts.

(3) A senior manager who was dismissed in December 20X0 commenced an action against the company alleging wrongful dismissal and claiming damages of £50,000. The company's solicitors estimate that the manager has a 25% chance of success in her claim. Irrecoverable legal costs of £10,000 will be incurred by Ochil regardless of the result of the action.

(4) Some years previously, Ochil Limited guaranteed the overdraft of an associated company, Sidlaw Limited, up to a limit of £100,000. Shortly after Ochil's balance sheet date, it was announced that Sidlaw was in financial difficulties and it is now probable that Ochil will have to meet the guarantee in full.

(5) In May 20X1 plans to merge Ochil with Cairngorm Limited were announced.

(6) It was discovered that an error was made in arriving at the stock figure at 31 March 20X1. Stock which had cost £30,000, with a net realisable value of £40,000, had been omitted.

Required

(a) Briefly explain the required accounting treatment of post balance sheet events and contingent liabilities according to SSAP 17 *Accounting for Post Balance Sheet Events* and FRS 12 *Provisions, Contingent Liabilities and Contingent Assets.* **(3 marks)**

(b) Apply the treatment you have stated in (a) to the six events (1) to (6) listed above in relation to the company's financial statements for the year ended 31 March 20X1. **(4 marks)**

(c) Prepare a statement showing the effect on the profit for the year of the adjustments required. **(3 marks)**

(Total : 10 marks)

Question 61

SSAP 13 (ACCA 12/00)

A company is engaged in a number of research and development projects. Under SSAP 13, state the conditions which must be met if development expenditure is to be capitalised.

(Total : 10 marks)

Question 62

Lomond (ACCA 12/00)

Lomond plc is engaged in a number of research and development projects. Its accounting policy as regards research and development is to capitalise expenditure as far as allowed by SSAP 13 *Accounting for Research and Development*. At 30 June 20X2, the following balances existed in the company's accounting records:

Project A — Development completed 30 June 20X0. Total expenditure £200,000. Being amortised over five years on the straight line basis. Balance at 30 June 20X2: £120,000.

Project B — A development project commenced 1 July 20X0. Total expenditure in the years ended 30 June 20X1 and 30 June 20X2 totalled £175,000. During the year ended 30 June 20X3 it became clear that a competitor had launched a superior product and the project was abandoned. Further development expenditure in the year ended 30 June 20X3 amounted to £55,000.

Project C — Development commenced 1 October 20X1. Expenditure to date:

Year ended 30 June 20X2	£85,000
Year ended 30 June 20X3	£170,000

All expenditure on Project C meets the criteria for capitalisation in SSAP 13.

Project D — In addition, research Project D commenced on 1 July 20X2. Expenditure to date (all on research):

Year ended 30 June 20X3	£80,000

Required

(a) On the basis that Lomond capitalises development expenditure to the maximum allowed by SSAP 13, calculate the amounts which should appear in the company's profit and loss account and balance sheet for research and development for the year ended 30 June 20X3. **(5 marks)**

(b) Show the notes which SSAP 13 requires in the financial statements for the year giving supporting figures for the items in the profit and loss account and balance sheet. **(5 marks)**

(Total : 10 marks)

Preparing Financial Statements (UK Stream)

Pilot Paper

Question Paper	
Time allowed	**3 hours**
This paper is divided into two sections	
Section A	ALL TWENTY FIVE questions are compulsory and MUST be attempted
Section B	ALL FIVE questions are compulsory and MUST be attempted

PILOT PAPER QUESTIONS

Section A

ALL questions are compulsory and MUST be attempted

Question 63 (Question 1 of Pilot Paper)

(i) In a sales ledger control account, which of the following lists is composed only of items which would appear on the credit side of the account?

A Cash received from customers, sales returns, bad debts written off, contras against amounts due to suppliers in the purchase ledger.

B Sales, cash refunds to customers, bad debts written off, discounts allowed.

C Cash received from customers, discounts allowed, interest charged on overdue accounts, bad debts written off.

D Sales, cash refunds to customers, interest charged on overdue accounts, contras against amounts due to suppliers in the purchase ledger.

(ii) Y purchased some plant on 1 January 2000 for £38,000. The payment for the plant was correctly entered in the cash book but was entered on the debit side of plant repairs account.

Y charges depreciation on the straight line basis at 20% per year, with a proportionate charge in the year of acquisition and assuming no scrap value at the end of the life of the asset.

How will Y's profit for the year ended 31 March 2000 be affected by the error?

A Understated by £30,400

B Understated by £36,100

C Understated by £38,000

D Overstated by £1,900

(iii) The trial balance of Z failed to agree, the totals being:

Debit	£836,200
Credit	£819,700

A suspense account was opened for the amount of the difference and the following errors were found and corrected:

1 The totals of the cash discount columns in the cash book had not been posted to the discount accounts. The figures were Discount Allowed £3,900 and Discount Received £5,100.

2 A cheque for £19,000 received from a customer was correctly entered in the cash book but was posted to the customer's account as £9,100.

What will the remaining balance on the suspense account be *after* the correction of these errors?

A £25,300 credit

B £7,700 credit

C £27,700 debit

D £5,400 credit

(iv) The trial balance of C Limited did not agree, and a suspense account was opened for the difference. Checking in the bookkeeping system revealed a number of errors.

1 £4,600 paid for motor van repairs was correctly treated in the cash book but was credited to motor vehicles asset account

2 £360 received from B, a customer, was credited in error to the account of BB

3 £9,500 paid for rent was debited to the rent account as £5,900

4 The total of the discount allowed column in the cash book had been debited in error to the discounts received account

5 No entries had been made to record a cash sale of £100.

Which of the errors above would require an entry to the suspense account as part of the process of correcting them?

A 3 and 4

B 1 and 3

C 2 and 5

D 2 and 3

(v) B acquired a lorry on 1 May 2000 at a cost of £30,000. The lorry has an estimated useful life of four years, and an estimated resale value at the end of that time of £6,000. B charges depreciation on the straight line basis, with a proportionate charge in the period of acquisition.

What will the depreciation charge for the lorry in B's account period to 30 September 2000?

A £3,000

B £2,500

C £2,000

D £5,000

(vi) SSAP 9 'Stocks and Long Term Contracts' defines the items that may be included in computing the value of a stock of finished goods manufactured by a business.

Which one of the following lists consists only of items which may be included in the balance sheet value of such stock, according to SSAP 9?

A Foreman's wages, carriage inwards, carriage outwards, raw materials

B Raw materials, carriage inwards, costs of storage of finished goods, plant depreciation

C Plant depreciation, carriage inwards, raw materials, foreman's wages

D Carriage outwards, raw materials, foreman's wages, plant depreciation.

(vii) The closing stock of X Limited amounted to £116,400 *excluding* the following two stock lines:

1 400 items which had cost £4 each. All were sold after the balance sheet date for £3 each, with selling expenses of £200 for the batch.

2 200 different items which had cost £30 each. These items were found to be defective at the balance sheet date. Rectification work after the balance sheet date amounted to £1,200, after which they were sold for £35 each, with selling expenses totalling £300.

Which of the following total figures should appear in the balance sheet of X for stock?

A £122,300

B £121,900

C £122,900

D £123,300

(viii) The Accounting Standards Board's 'Statement of Principles for Financial Reporting' gives five qualitative characteristics which make financial information reliable.

These five characteristics are:

A Prudence, consistency, understandability, faithful representation, substance over form.

B Accruals basis, going concern concept, consistency, prudence, true and fair view.

C Faithful representation, neutrality, substance over form, completeness, consistency

D Freedom from material error, prudence, faithful representation, neutrality, completeness.

(ix) The following attempt at a bank reconciliation statement has been prepared by Q Limited:

	£
Overdraft per bank statement	38,600
Add: deposits not credited	41,200
	79,800
Less: outstanding cheques	3,300
Overdraft per cash book	76,500

Assuming the bank statement balance of £38,600 to be correct, what *should* the cash book balance be?

A £76,500 overdrawn, as stated

B £5,900 overdrawn

C £700 overdrawn

D £5,900 cash at bank

(x) After checking a business cash book against the bank statement, which of the following items could require an entry in the cash book?

1 Bank charges
2 A cheque from a customer which was dishonoured
3 Cheque not presented
4 Deposits not credited
5 Credit transfer entered in bank statement
6 Standing order entered in bank statement.

A 1, 2, 5 and 6

B 3 and 4

C 1, 3, 4 and 6

D 3, 4, 5 and 6

(xi) The following information is relevant to the calculation of the sales figure for Alpha, a sole trader who does not keep proper accounting records:

	£
Opening debtors	29,100
Cash received from credit customers and paid into the bank	381,600
Expenses paid out of cash received from credit customers before banking	6,800
Bad debts written off	7,200
Refunds to credit customers	2,100
Discounts allowed to credit customers	9,400
Cash sales	112,900
Closing debtors	38,600

The figure which should appear in Alpha's trading account for sales is:

A £525,300

B £511,700

C £529,500

D £510,900

(xii) A sole trader who does not keep full accounting records wishes to calculate her sales revenue for the year.

The information available is:

1	Opening stock	£17,000
2	Closing stock	£24,000
3	Purchases	£91,000
4	Standard gross profit percentage on sales revenue	40%

Which of the following is the sales figure for the year calculated from these figures?

A £117,600

B £108,000

C £210,000

D £140,000

(xiii) A business compiling its accounts for the year to 31 January each year pays rent quarterly in advance on 1 January, 1 April, 1 July and 1 October each year. After remaining unchanged for some years, the rent was increased from £24,000 per year to £30,000 per year as from 1 July 2000.

Which of the following figures is the rent expense which should appear in the profit and loss account for the year ended 31 January 2001?

A £27,500

B £29,500

C £28,000

D £29,000

(xiv) On 31 December 2000 the stock of V Limited was destroyed by fire. The following information is available:

1 Stock at 1 December 2000 at cost £28,400

2 Purchases for December 2000 £49,600

3 Sales for December 2000 £64,800

4 Standard gross profit percentage on sales revenue 30%.

Based on this information, which of the following is the amount of stock destroyed?

A £45,360

B £32,640

C £40,971

D £19,440

(xv) Which of the following statements concerning the accounting treatment of research and development expenditure are true, according to SSAP 13 'Accounting for Research and Development'?

1 If certain criteria are met, research expenditure may be recognised as an asset.

2 Research expenditure, other than capital expenditure on research facilities, should be recognised as an expense incurred.

3 In deciding whether development expenditure qualifies to be recognised as an asset, it is necessary to consider whether there will be adequate finance available to complete the project.

4 Development expenditure recognised as an asset must be amortised over a period not exceeding five years.

5 The financial statements should disclose the total amount of research and development expenditure recognised as an expense during the period.

A 1, 4 and 5

B 2, 4 and 5

C 2, 3 and 4

D 2, 3 and 5

(xvi) D, E and F are in partnership, sharing profits in the ratio 5:3:2 respectively, after charging salaries for E and F of £24,000 per year.

On 1 July 2000 they agreed to change the profit-sharing ratio to 3:1:1 and to increase E's salary to £36,000 per year, F's salary continuing unchanged.

For the year ended 31 December 2000 the partnership profit amounted to £480,000.

Which of the following correctly states the partners' total profit shares for the year?

	D	*E*	*F*
A	£234,000	£136,800	£109,200
B	£213,000	£157,800	£109,200
C	£186,000	£171,600	£122,400
D	£237,600	£132,000	£110,400

(xvii) At 1 January 2000 the capital structure of Q Limited was as follows:

	£
Issued share capital 1,000,000 ordinary shares of 50p each	500,000
Share premium account	300,000

On 1 April 2000 the company made an issue of 200,000 50p shares at £1.30 each, and on 1 July the company made a bonus (capitalisation) issue of one share for every four in issue at the time, using the share premium account for the purpose.

Which of the following correctly states the company's share capital and share premium account at 31 December 2000?

	Share capital	*Share premium account*
A	£750,000	£230,000
B	£875,000	£285,000
C	£750,000	£310,000
D	£750,000	£610,000

(xviii) A company compiles its accounts for the year to 31 March. In May 2000 the company sold its northern division, making a profit of £4m. The company's trading profit for the year to 31 March 2000 was £11m, to which the northern division had contributed £3m.

Which of the following treatments of the profit on the sale of the northern division and of its trading results is correct according to FRS 3 'Reporting Financial Performance'?

	Trading results of northern division in profit and loss account for year ended 31 March 2000 as:	*Profit on sale of northern division In profit and loss account as an exceptional item separately disclosed for year ended:*
A	Discontinuing activity	31 March 2000
B	Discontinuing activity	31 March 2001
C	Part of continuing activities	31 March 2000
D	Part of continuing activities	31 March 2001

(xix) FRS 1 'Cash Flow Statements' requires the cash flow statement to be accompanied by a note reconciling operating profit to net operating cash flow.

Which of the following lists consists only of items which could appear in such a reconciliation?

A Depreciation, increase in debtors, decrease in creditors, interest paid, increase in stocks

B Increase in creditors, decrease in stocks, profit on sale of plant, depreciation, decrease in debtors

C Increase in creditors, equity dividends paid, depreciation, decrease in debtors, increase in stocks

D Depreciation, interest paid, equity dividends paid, decrease in stocks.

(xx) SSAP 17 'Accounting for Post Balance Sheet Events' regulates the extent to which events after the balance sheet date should be reflected in financial statements.

Which of the following lists of such events consists only of items that, according to SSAP 17, should normally be classified as non-adjusting?

A Insolvency of a debtor whose balance was outstanding at the balance sheet date, issue of shares or debentures, a major merger with another company

B Issue of shares or debentures, changes in foreign exchange rates, major purchases of fixed assets

C A major merger with another company, destruction of a major fixed asset by fire, discovery of fraud or error which shows that the financial statements were incorrect

D Sale of stock giving evidence about its value at the balance sheet date, issue of shares or debentures, destruction of a major fixed asset by fire.

(xxi) An analysis of its financial statements revealed that the debtor collection period of R Limited was 100 days, when 60 days is a reasonable figure.

Which one of the following could NOT account for the high level of 100 days?

A Poor performance in R's credit control department

B A large credit sale made just before the balance sheet date

C R's trade is seasonal

D A downturn in R's trade in the last quarter of the year.

(xxii) Which of the following correctly defines working capital?

A Fixed assets plus current assets minus current liabilities

B Current assets minus current liabilities

C Fixed assets plus current assets

D Share capital plus reserves.

(xxiii) At 1 January 1998 H Limited acquired 80% of the share capital of S for £160,000. At that date the share capital consisted of 100,000 ordinary shares of £1 each and its reserves totalled £40,000. Goodwill on acquisition of subsidiaries is amortised on the straight line basis over five years.

In the consolidated balance sheet of H and its subsidiary S at 31 December 2000 the amount appearing for goodwill should be:

A £16,000

B £19,200

C £28,800

D £4,000

(xxiv) At 1 January 1998 H Limited acquired 60% of the share capital of S for £180,000. At that date the share capital of S consisted of 200,000 shares of 50p each. The reserves of H and S are stated below:

	At 1 January 1998	*At 31 December 2000*
	£	*£*
H	280,000	340,000
S	50,000	180,000

In the consolidated balance sheet of H and its subsidiary S at 31 December 2000, what amount should appear for the minority interest in S?

A £92,000

B £280,000

C £152,000

D £112,000

(xxv) H Limited acquired 75% of the share capital of S for £280,000 on 1 January 1994. Goodwill arising on consolidation has been fully amortised.

Details of the share capital and reserves of S are as follows:

	At 1 January 1994	*At 31 December 2000*
	£	*£*
Share capital	200,000	200,000
Profit and loss account reserve	120,000	180,000

At 31 December 2000 the profit and loss account reserve of H amounted to £480,000.

What figure should appear in the consolidated balance sheet of H and S for the profit and loss account reserve at 31 December 2000?

A £530,000

B £525,000

C £485,000

D £575,000

Section B

All questions are compulsory and MUST be attempted

Question 64 (Question 2 of Pilot Paper)

If the information *in* financial statements is to be useful, regard must be had to the following *accounting concepts among others:*

(a) Materiality **(4 marks)**

(b) Substance over form **(3 marks)**

(c) Money measurement **(3 marks)**

Required:

Explain the meaning of each of these concepts, including in your explanations one example of the application of each of them. **(Total : 10 marks)**

Question 65 (Question 3 of Pilot Paper)

The balance sheets of Brood Limited, as at 30 April 2000 and 30 April 2001 are given below:

		30 April 2000		*30 April 2001*
	£000	*£000*	*£000*	*£000*
Assets				
Tangible fixed assets				
Cost or valuation	51,000		63,000	
Accumulated depreciation	(12,500)	38,500	(16,300)	46,700
Current Assets				
Stocks	16,400		18,400	
Trade debtors	19,100		20,600	
Sundry debtors and prepayments	3,100		4,000	
Total Assets	38,600		43,000	
Less: Current liabilities				
Trade creditors	(11,400)		(8,400)	
Accruals	(3,400)		(4,200)	
Overdraft at bank	(13,700)		(4,800)	
	28,500		17,400	
Net current assets		10,100		25,600
		48,600		72,300
Less: 7% Debentures (£20m issued 1 May 2000)		(20,000)		(40,000)
		28,600		32,300

Called up share capital	10,000	10,000
Share premium account	5,000	5,000
Revaluation reserve	5,000	5,000
Profit and loss account	8,600	12,300
	28,600	32,300

The summarised profit and loss accounts of Brood for the years ended 30 April 2000 and 2001, ignoring tax, are:

	Year ended 30 April *2000* *£000*	*2001* *£000*
Sales	58,000	66,000
Cost of sales	(43,000)	(49,000)
Gross profit	15,000	17,000
Operating expenses	(10,000)	(10,500)
Profit from operations	5,000	6,500
Interest payable	(1,400)	(2,800)
Net profit for the period	3,600	3,700

Required:

(a) Calculate the following ratios for each of the two years:

(i) Return on total capital employed

(ii) Return on owners' equity

(iii) Current ratio

(iv) Quick ratio (acid test)

(v) Gearing (leverage)

Use year-end figures for all ratios. **(5 marks)**

(b) Comment briefly on the movements in these ratios between the two years. **(5 marks)**

(Total : 10 marks)

Question 66 (Question 4 of Pilot Paper)

The balance sheets of Crash Limited at 31 March 2000 and 31 March 2001 were as follows:

		31 March			
		2000		*2001*	
	Reference to notes	*£000*	*£000*	*£000*	*£000*
Fixed assets	1				
Cost or valuation		9,000		10,950	
Accumulated depreciation		(3,300)	5,700	(3,600)	7,350
Current assets					
Stock		1,215		1,350	
Debtors		1,350		1,290	
Cash		60		105	
Total assets		2,625		2,745	
Less: Current liabilities					
Trade creditors		(990)		(1,080)	
Bank overdraft		(195)		(270)	
		(1,185)		(1,350)	
			1,440		1,395
Net current assets			7,140		8,745
Less: 10% debentures			(1,500)		(750)
			5,640		7,995
Called up share capital			2,250		3,000
Share premium account			750		1,200
Revaluation reserve			-		750
Profit and loss account			2,640		3,045
			5,640		7,995

Notes:

1 Fixed assets

(a) During the year fixed assets, which had cost £1,500,000 and which had a book value of £300,000 at 31 March 2000, were sold for £375,000.

(b) Land acquired in 1997 was revalued upwards by £750,000 in preparing the balance sheet at 31 March 2001.

2 Debentures

Interest is due half-yearly on 30 September and 31 March and was paid on the due dates. The company repaid £750,000 debentures on 31 March 2001.

3 Profit before interest for the year ended 31 March 2001 was £555,000. No dividends were paid during the year.

4 Ignore taxation.

Required:

Prepare a cash flow statement for Crash for the year ended 31 March 2001 using the indirect method, complying as far as possible with the requirements of FRS 1 'Cash Flow Statements'.

The note reconciling net cash flow with movement in net debt is NOT required.

(Total : 10 marks)

Question 67 (Question 5 of Pilot Paper)

The directors of Jurien Limited are considering the draft financial statements for the year ended 31 March 2001.

Matters under discussion are:

(a) After a party in February 2000, eighteen people died as a result of food poisoning from eating food manufactured by Jurien. At 31 March 2001 the company was advised that there was probably no liability and the matter was disclosed as a contingent liability at that date. As the result of developments in the case, which is still not settled, the company was advised that it is now probable, as at 31 March 2001, that the company will be found liable. Some directors consider that the matter should remain a contingent liability until the court case decides the matter, while others consider that provision should be made for it in the financial statements for the year ended 31 March 2001. **(3 marks)**

(b) No provision has yet been made for a trade debtor of £560,000 outstanding at 31 March 2001. In June 2001 the directors of Jurien became aware that the debtor was in financial difficulties. Directors are divided as to whether a provision should be made or not. **(3 marks)**

(c) The company's closing stock of finished goods is valued by taking the cost of labour and materials plus an allocation of overheads. One director has queried the basis on which overheads are added and has asked for clarification of the relevant rules, with two examples of overheads which must be excluded. **(4 marks)**

Required:

Write a memorandum to the directors advising them on the three points raised, explaining the authority for your advice in each case. **(10 marks)**

Question 68 (Question 6 of Pilot Paper)

The following extracts have been taken from the trial balance of Pride Limited at 31 March 2001:

		£000	*£000*
Issued share capital			
500,000 ordinary shares of 50p each			250
Share premium account 1 April 2000			180
Profit and loss account 31 March 2001			34
Land at cost		210	
Buildings	- cost 1 April 2000	200	
	- accumulated depreciation at 1 April 2000		120
Plant and equipment	- cost	318	
	- accumulated depreciation at 1 April 2000		88
Debtors		146	
Cash at bank		50	
Creditors			94
10% debentures issued 1995			100
Allowance for doubtful debts			10
Suspense account			166

Notes:

1 The profit and loss account balance of £34,000 shown above is the final balance of retained profit for the year and may be incorporated into your answer as such.

2 The balance on the suspense account is made up as follows:

	£000
Receipt of cash on 8 January 2001 on the issue of 200,000 ordinary shares of 50p each at a premium of 30p per share	160
Proceeds of sale of plant*	6
	166

* The plant had originally cost £18,000 and had been written down to £6,000 at 31 March 2000. The company's policy is to provide depreciation for a full year in the year of acquisition of assets and none in the year of sale.

3 Depreciation is to be provided for on the straight line basis at the following annual rates:

Land	Nil
Buildings	2%
Plant and equipment	20%

4 The provision for doubtful debts is to be increased to £12,000.

5 Prepayments and accruals at 31 March 2001 were:

	£000
Prepayments	8,000
Accruals	4,000

6 The closing stock was £180,000.

Required:

Prepare the balance sheet of Pride Limited as at 31 March 2001 for publication complying as far as possible with the provisions of the Companies Acts. **(10 marks)**

Multiple choice answers

1 D

The owner is a completely separate entity to the business therefore if he takes goods from stock for his own personal use these must be treated as drawings and purchases correspondingly reduced.

---

2 D

Reconstruction of cost of goods sold to establish the purchases figure:

Opening stock		12,000	
Add: Purchases	122,000		found by diff
Less: Returns	(5,000)	117,000	
Closing stock		(18,000)	
Cost of goods sold		111,000	

---

3 A

Reconstruction of the bank account

Balance b/fwd	2,500	Payment (1,000 - 20%) - 10%	720
Receipt (200 - 5%)	190	Balance c/fwd (diff)	1,970
	2,690		2,690

---

4 C

---

5 B

---

6 C

---

7 D

Opening balance sheet and adjustments required:

Assets (cash)	1,000	Liabilities (capital)	1,000
Transaction 1 (stock)	800	Creditor	800
Transaction 2 (cash)	1,175	VAT owing	175
Stock	(400)	Profit (add to capital) (1,000 - (½ × 800))	600
Closing balance	2,575		2,575

Therefore Assets 2,575 less Liabilities 975 = Capital 1,600.

---

8 B

Opening capital	10,000
Introduced	4,000
Drawings	(8,000)
Loss - balancing figure	(1,500)
Closing capital	4,500

---

9 C

Profit	8,000
Add back depreciation	12,000
Net cash inflow	20,000
Purchase of F A	(25,000)
Decrease	(5,000)

This is the only combination which takes you from £8,000 profit to a decrease in cash of £5,000.

---

10 B

Reconstruction of T & P & L Account:

	£	
Sales	2,400	100%
Cost of sales	1,600	66 ⅔ %
Gross profit	800	33 ⅓ %
Expenses	680	
Net profit	120	ie 5%

---

11 B

	£
Preference dividend for year 5% of £100,000	5,000
Ordinary dividend for year 20p × 400,000 shares	80,000
Total dividend is	85,000

---

12 A

Without knowing or being able to calculate the net book value of the asset, neither the sale proceeds nor the length of ownership can be determined.

---

13 C

Typically small immaterial items will be written off to the profit and loss account despite being used in the business for some considerable time.

---

14 A

	Plant register		*Ledger*
	£		£
1 July 1997	47,500	Cost	60,000
Amendment (4,000 + 1,500)	(5,500)	Depreciation	(15,000)
Revised figure	42,000	NBV	45,000

ie the plant register is £3,000 lower than the ledger.

---

15 B

	£
Balance as per bank statement	(800)
Unpresented cheque	(80)
Balance to show in balance sheet	(880)

---

16 D

---

17 C

---

18 D

---

19 B

---

20 A

Motor expenses account

1/9	Balance b/fwd	80	1/9	Balance b/fwd	95
	Bank	95	30/9	P & L account	385*
	Bank	245			
30/9	Balance c/fwd	120	30/9	Balance c/fwd	60
		540			540

* ie the balancing figure.

Make sure that you include the closing balance for 3 months insurance prepaid.

---

21 A

	£
List price	800
Trade discount (20%)	(160)
	640
Cash or settlement discount (5%)	(32)
Cheque to settle	608

Therefore the bookkeeping entries are:

	£	£
Debit PQ Ltd (the debtor)	640	
Credit sales account		640
Debit bank account	608	
Debit discount allowed account	32	
Credit PQ Ltd		640

22 B

Year 1 :	2,400 - 480	=	1,920
Year 2 :	1,920 - 384	=	1,536
Year 3 :	1,536 - 307.20	=	1,228.80

Book value at time of sale = £1,228.80

∴ Loss of £28.80

23 C

Summarised stock record file

					£
1/8/97	Opening balance	30 × £2.00			60
5/8/97	Purchase	50 × £2.40	=	(120)	180
10/8/97	Issue	40 × (180/80)	=	(90)	90
18/8/97	Purchase	60 × £2.50	=	(150)	240
23/8/97	Issue	25 × (240/100)	=	(60)	180

24 B

Reconstruction of the trading account:

	£	£
Sales		148,000
Opening stock	34,000	
Purchases	100,000	
	134,000	
Closing stock*	26,000	108,000
Gross profit		40,000

* ie the balancing figure.

25 D

	£	%
Sales	180,000	150
Cost of sales	120,000	100
Gross profit	60,000	5

$\therefore$ Cost of sales = £120,000

Average stock = $\frac{12,000 + 18,000}{2}$ = 15,000

Therefore stock turnover is $\frac{120,000}{15,000}$ = 8 times

26 D

27 C

28 D

29 C

Reconstruction of the trading account:

	£	£
Sales		40,000
Returns inwards		(2,000)
		38,000
Opening stock	3,000	
Purchases	20,000	
Returns outwards	(4,000)	
Closing stock	(3,000)	(16,000)
Gross profit		22,000

VAT is not included in sales, purchases or returns.

---

30 B

	£
Original cash book figure	2,490
Adjustment re charges	(50)
Adjustment re dishonoured cheque	(140)
	2,300

---

31 A

	£000
Profit for the year	1,175
Add back depreciation	100
	1,275
Add: Issue of shares	1,000
Less: Repayment of debentures	(750)
Less: Purchase of fixed assets	(200)
	1,325
Less: Increase in working capital	(575)
Increase in bank balance	750

You need to reconstruct the cash flow statement and then work back up to the profit figure.

---

32 D

---

33 C

	£
Capital at 1/4/97	6,500
Add: Profit (after drawings)	32,500
Less: VAT element	(70)
Capital at 31/5/98	38,930

34 B

Only development expenditure can be capitalised. All research costs must be written off to the profit and loss account.

35 A

$$\frac{\text{Cost of sales}}{\text{Average stock}} = \frac{£24{,}500}{(4{,}000+6{,}000)\div 2} = 4.9 \text{ times}$$

36 A

37 C

Current ratio is 2,900 : 1,100 = 2.6 : 1 ie High

Acid test ratio is 1,000 : 1,100 = 0.9 : 1 ie Acceptable

A very difficult question to answer as all answers given are correct and the correct answer is a matter of opinion.

38 C

	£
Sales were	100,800
Cost of sales was	(72,000)
∴ Gross profit	28,800

$$\text{Gross profit mark up} = \frac{£28{,}800}{£72{,}000} \times 100 = 40\%$$

39 D

Answers A and B would increase revenue reserves. Answer C increases a capital reserve.

40 A

	£
Opening balance	34,500
Credit purchases	78,400
Discounts	(1,200)
Payments	(68,900)
Purchase returns	(4,700)
	38,100

41 B

Diesel fuel creditor account		*Cost of fuel used*	
	£		£
Balance b/fwd	(1,700)	Opening stock	12,500
Payments	85,400	Purchases	85,000
Balance c/fwd	1,300	Closing stock	(9,800)
Purchases	85,000	Charge in P/L	87,700

42 C

	Qty	*Value* £	*Average cost* £
1 October (60 × 12)	60	720	12
8 October (40 × 15)	100	1,320	13.20
14 October (50 × 18)	150	2,220	14.80
21 October (75 × 14.80)	75	1,110	

43 A

	£	
9,000 × 0.7 × 0.7 × 0.7 =	3,087	(NBV)
Proceeds of sale	(3,000)	
Loss on disposal	87	

44 D

45 B

46 A

Current ratio	=	1,390 : 420 = 3.3 : 1	(ie high)
Acid test	=	420 : 420 = 1 : 1	(ie ideal)

47 C

$$\frac{\text{PBIT} \times 100}{\text{Ave cap}} \qquad \frac{1{,}200 \times 100}{(11{,}200 + 11{,}800)/2} = 10.43\%$$

Note that the balance sheet given is the opening balance sheet.

48 C

49 B

Profit is overstated since depreciation is charged based on the historical cost of the fixed assets.

50 C

51 D

52 B

	£	
Statement balance	13,400	
Add back dishonoured cheque	300	
Add back bank charges	50	
Less: Unpresented cheques	(1,400)	
Adjustment re error	(390)	ie twice 195
	11,960	

53 C

54 D

	£
Stationery	14.10
Travel	25.50
Refreshments	12.90
Sundry creditors (£24 × 1.175)	28.20
	80.70

55 A

	£
Cashbook balance	(1,240)
Unpresented cheques	450
Receipt not yet processed	(140)
Bank charges	(75)
As per statement	(1,005)

56 C

57 A

	£	
£5,000 × 0.8 × 0.8 × 0.8 =	2,560	(ie WDV)
Receipt	(2,200)	
Loss on disposal	360	

58 B

Summarised stock card

				£
6 × 15				90
10 × 19.80	=	198	16	288
10 × 18	=	(180)	6	108
20 × 24.50	=	490	26	598
5 × 23	=	(115)	21	483

Trading account

		£
Sales 15 × 30		450
Op. stock	90	
Purchase	688	
Cl. stock	(483)	(295)
Profit		155

Note: Issues are shown in brackets.

59 A

60 A

61 D

62 B

	£
Balance as per ledger account	260 cr
Add back discount	80 cr
Returned goods not yet processed	270 cr
Payment not yet processed by supplier	830 cr
Therefore balance on statement should be	1,440
Actual balance on statement	1,350
Unexplained difference	90

63 D

Answer B is incorrect as the cash flow statement is not limited to operating activities.

64 A

Suspense account

	£		£
Difference per TB	500	Provision for bad debts	840
Sales account	150		
Balance	190		
	840		840

The rent received has been credited correctly in the accounts but to the wrong account.

65 C

	£
Catalogue price	1,000
20% trade discount	(200)
Purchase cost on 1/11/99	800

No entries are made for the cash discount until payment is actually made.

66 B

Control account

	£		£
Opening balance	14,500	Returns inwards	1,400
Credit sales	53,500	Contra	500
		Discounts allowed	350
		Receipts	51,200
		Balance c/fwd	14,550
	68,000		68,000

67 C

68 A

Gearing at 31/10/98 = $\frac{20}{40} \times 100$ = 50%

Gearing at 31/10/99 = $\frac{40}{60} \times 100$ = 67%

ie gearing has increased.

69 B

Rate of stockturn = $\frac{\text{Cost of sales}}{\text{Average stock}}$

Rate of stockturn y/e 31/10/98 = $\frac{1{,}250}{80}$ = 15.6

Rate of stockturn y/e 31/10/99 = $\frac{1{,}300}{100}$ = 13

ie the rate of stockturn has decreased.

As the stock is being held for longer, capital is tied up in it for longer, therefore having a possible detrimental effect on liquidity.

70 C

71 B

72 A

73 D

	£
Balance as per sales ledger control	37,642
Deduct incorrect posting of cash discount	(1,802)
	35,840

Answers A and B would increase the balance on the sales ledger control account. Correction of answer C would decrease the sales ledger total.

74 A

75 D

	£
Original cost	64,000
Depreciation 31/12/96	(32,000)
NBV 31/12/96	32,000
Depreciation 31/12/97	(16,000)
NBV 31/12/97	16,000
Depreciation 31/12/98	(8,000)
NBV 31/12/98	8,000
Depreciation 31/12/99	(4,000)
NBV 31/12/99	4,000

Machine sold for £2,500 so there is a loss of £1,500.

76 C

77 B

(80) + 2,145 + 120 = 2,185

The line rental can be ignored as it has not changed in value and four rental charges are included in the bills of £2,145.

78 B

	£	£
Closing capital was		19,000
Increase in the year was:		
Profit	8,000	
Capital introduced	9,800	
Drawings	(4,200)	(13,600)
Therefore opening capital was		5,400

---

79 D

	£
Original profit figure	18,750
Add back depreciation charge	1,250
Purchase of fixed assets	(8,000)
Increase in debtors	(1,000)
Decrease in stocks	1,800
Increase in creditors	350
Increase in cash	13,150

---

80 A

If FIFO is used, rather than weighted average cost, then cost of sales will use older prices and therefore be lower, this will cause higher profit and closing stock will be valued at the most recent purchase price which will be higher than at average cost.

---

81 C

	£
Revised sales (£130,000 × 1.4)	182,000
Revised COS (£60,000 × 2)	(120,000)
Gross profit	62,000

$$\text{Mark up} = \frac{62{,}000}{120{,}000} = 51.7\%$$

---

82 C

An increased bank balance would not account for the fall in acid test ratio. A decreased bank balance would not account for the increased current ratio. Increases in debtors and creditors would cancel each other out.

Answers

Answer 1

Statement of Principles

> *Tutorial note:*
>
> This question asked for the thinking behind the ASB's Statement of Principles, followed by specific explanations.
>
> **Not required** - General discussion on the Statement of Principles.

(a) The ASB recognised the weakness of the piecemeal approach to standard setting and developed the Statement of Principles which is effectively a conceptual framework.

The purposes of the Statement of Principles are:

(i) to set out the principles that the ASB believes should underlie the preparation and presentation of financial statements.

(ii) to provide a frame of reference to be used by the ASB in the development of future accounting standards.

(iii) to clarify the conceptual underpinnings of proposed standards.

(iv) to provide information about the ASB's approach to the formulation of standards.

(v) to assist preparers and users of financial statements in applying standards.

(b) (i) **Materiality**

Materiality is a threshold quality. If information could influence users' decisions taken on the basis of financial statements, it is **material**.

(ii) **Relevance**

Financial information is **relevant** if it can assist users' decision-making by helping them to evaluate past, present or future events or confirming, or correcting, their existing evaluations.

(iii) **Reliability**

To be **reliable**, information must be free from bias and error. Other qualities which make information reliable include faithful representation, neutrality, completeness and prudence.

Answer 2

User groups

(a) **Shareholders**

Shareholders need information about the level of risk and return associated with their investment. This information will help them to decide whether to keep or dispose of their shares. Specifically, shareholders will want to know about a company's ability to pay out dividends.

Management

Management make day-to-day decisions on how to control various scarce resources. Relevant information will help them to predict outcomes of likely scenarios so that they may choose the most appropriate course of action.

Employees

Employees want information concerning job security such as the financial profitability and liquidity of the company. Also if they have company pensions they would want to know how the relevant company assets are being managed.

(b) Shareholders and employees are both interested in long-term stability and profitability but because of the historical nature of the information used to prepare financial statements, there is doubt about the relevance of the information for these user groups.

Published financial statements are not designed to provide information for management. Their information needs are catered for by internally generated management accounts which are far more predictive in nature.

Answer 3

Owner of a business (ACCA 12/00)

> ***Tutorial note:***
>
> This question requires five differences between the two methods of operating a business. You should ensure that you explain the key factors first followed by less important ones.
>
> **Not required** - General discussion on how each business is managed.

Any five from the following:

	Sole trader	**Limited company**
Legal entity	The business is not separate from the owner.	Companies are separate legal entities in law – they can sue and be sued.
Ownership	The business is owned by the sole trader.	The company is owned by shareholders.
Legal control	Little statutory control.	Companies must comply with company rules being governed by the Companies Acts.

Liability	Sole trader has unlimited liability to creditors.	The liability of shareholders is limited to the capital already introduced by them.
Constitution	No formal constitution required.	The objects, powers and duties of a company must be set out in its memorandum and articles of association.
Audit	An audit is not required.	An audit is required (unless exempt as a small company) which is a substantial cost.
Management	By the owner	Separation of management (by directors) from ownership (by the shareholders).
Returns	The owner takes all the profit of the business.	The owners (shareholders) may receive dividends out of the profits of the business.
Transfer of ownership	By transfer of the business itself	By transfer of the shares rather than the business itself.

Answer 4

Historical cost accounting (ACCA 12/97)

> ***Tutorial note:***
>
> This question does not require a lengthy description of historical cost accounting, but an explanation of four specific points.

Distortions of financial statements by the use of historical cost accounting

(i) **The balance sheet**

This will not actually represent the value of the business. Where prices are rising because of inflation, valuing an asset at net book value may lead to a major understatement of its value. This is because net book value is a depreciated historical cost.

(ii) **Depreciation**

The depreciation charge will normally be based on historical cost which means that the charge in the profit and loss account will not show the actual benefit of using the asset, ie the expense is understated. This in turn can lead to an overstatement of profit.

(iii) **Profit on disposal of fixed assets**

Profit on disposal is based on historical cost, comparing proceeds to net book value. Where inflation is causing rising prices, the goods sold will cost more to replace. This will lead to the depletion of physical capital and overstated profit.

(iv) **Interpretation**

Performance ratios such as return on capital employed can be distorted. This distortion comes from two factors. Profit is overstated as a result of the depreciation charge and any profit on disposal and capital employed is understated in the value of fixed assets.

Note that the examiner requires four respects of the distortions caused by historical cost accounting. The four (and only four) given should cover different areas to be awarded the available marks.

Answer 5

Limitations of HCA (ACCA 12/97)

(i) Historical cost accounting is an easily understandable economic system whereas alternatives tend to be more complicated and expensive.

(ii) Revaluations in historical cost accounting help to reduce the distortions in the balance sheet. These are generally permitted.

(iii) Other methods rely heavily on valuation, which can be subjective, whereas the historical cost is objective and can be easily verified by inspecting the original invoice.

(iv) As historical cost accounting (and its limitations and distortions) is well understood, users make allowances for such distortions in the value of fixed assets.

Answer 6

Accounting concepts (ACCA 12/97 amended)

> ***Tutorial note:***
>
> This question required definitions of fairly well-known concepts.

Neutrality

This is the same as objectivity. Financial statements should be as objective as possible. Transactions are to be recorded objectively as historical events. In other words, it is the intention that financial statements should be free from bias.

For example, the decision as to whether or not a provision is to be made against a doubtful debt should not be influenced by its impact upon the company's ability to continue to trade.

Money measurement

This concept states that only assets and liabilities that are capable of being measured in monetary terms will be included in the balance sheet of a company.

For example, inherent goodwill, such as customer loyalty that has built up over a long period of time, is an asset to a company but it cannot be measured in monetary terms with any degree of precision.

Accruals

This concept states that income should be matched with related expenditure and that both income and expenditure should be included in the profit and loss account in the period in which it is incurred. The period when items are paid or received are not relevant here.

For example, electricity is billed in arrears so an additional accrual will be required at the end of an accounting period in order to account correctly for the amount that remains unbilled.

Substance over form

The economic substance of a transaction is the main factor in deciding the treatment of an item in the financial statements. The substance of a transaction is more important than its legal form.

For example, an asset purchased under a hire purchase agreement is treated as being owned by the company buying the asset as soon as the deposit is paid although, legally, ownership transfers only after all payments have been made.

Consistency

A business should be consistent in its accounting treatment of similar items, both within a particular accounting period and between one accounting period and the next.

For example, the depreciation policy of a company regarding the way in which the cost of tangible fixed assets is spread over their estimated useful lives should be consistent (the same each year) unless there is a very good reason for changing it.

The five accounting concepts required are fundamental to the accounting framework and should have provided easy marks. Note that the question also required an explanation of the relevance of the concepts. An example in each case would gain the available marks.

Answer 7

Conflict of concepts

(i) **Accruals v prudence**

The accruals/matching concept states that income may be accrued in order to smooth out the way in which it is actually received.

Prudence states that income and profits should not be anticipated and the conflict is resolved by allowing prudence to prevail.

(ii) **Consistency v prudence**

If consistency clashes with prudence then, again, prudence should prevail.

For example, the consistent capitalisation of development expenditure is acceptable until such time as the relevant criteria are no longer met. If this occurs, then prudence dictates that all previously capitalised expenditure should be written off.

Note that the two examples given cover clashes between ***different*** *concepts. If you restrict your examples to the same conflict, you will only gain half the marks.*

Answer 8

Ermine (ACCA 12/99)

> *Tutorial note:*
>
> This question relates to capital maintenance and historical cost accounting. This is standard theory and should be thoroughly understood. Ensure that you relate the theory to the scenario given.

The financial capital of a business comprises its capital measured in monetary terms. Ermine commenced trading on 1 July 20X8 with capital of £100,000 cash and ended the year with the same cash. Ermine has therefore maintained the financial capital of the business.

The physical capital of a business comprises its capital measured in non-monetary terms. The £100,000 cash at the end of the year would not be sufficient to purchase the same amount of stock as it did at the beginning of the year. Ermine has not therefore maintained his physical capital.

If the whole of a business' profit is withdrawn by the trader (as Ermine has done), in times of rising prices, the financial capital will not buy the same stock and other assets to enable the business to continue operating at the same level.

This illustrates one of the disadvantages of historical cost accounting.

Answer 9

HCA (ACCA 12/99)

(a) Three ways in which the use of historical cost accounting may cause financial statements to be misleading:

(i) **Depreciation**
Under a system of historical cost accounting, the purpose of depreciation is simply to allocate the original cost of a fixed asset over its estimated useful life. When inflation is taken into account, the depreciation provision at the end of the asset's useful life will fall short of its replacement cost.

(ii) **Stock and cost of sales**
During a period of inflation the effect of valuing stock on a historical cost basis using the FIFO method is to overstate the real profit of a business, since sales (in current terms) are matched with cost of sales (in historical terms). If the whole of the historical cost profit is distributed, the business would not be maintaining the capital of the business intact in real terms.

(iii) **Comparability of data over time**
Users of accounts need to be able to compare the results of the business over a number of years so that trends can be identified. Even if the financial statements show that sales have increased over time, the increase may not match the rate of inflation over that same period. In that case there has been a real decline in sales rather than an increase.

(b) Advantages of historical cost accounting:

(i) The records are based on objective and verifiable amounts (actual cost of stock, assets, etc) and do not rely on subjective valuations.
(ii) It is simple and cheap.
(iii) The historical cost concept is well understood and widely accepted.

Answer 10

Concepts (ACCA 6/00)

> ***Tutorial note:***
>
> This question covered standard book work on accounting concepts and should have provided easy marks.
>
> **Not required** - Definition of accounting concepts other than those specifically mentioned.

(a) **Money measurement**: Accounts only record items to which a monetary value can be attributed. Not all items can be measured owing to the practical difficulties of valuation.

Example – it may be desirable to value employees and record them as an asset on the balance sheet but it is difficult to arrive at a value. According to the money measurement concept, financial accounting would not recognise the worth of employees.

(b) **Substance over form**: The economic substance of a transaction should be reflected in the accounts, rather than simply its legal form.

Example – assets acquired on hire purchase terms are not owned by the user until the final instalment has been paid. However, such fixed assets are recorded in the user's accounts at the start of the hire purchase agreement, since the substance of the transaction is that the accounts should reflect the use of a fixed asset in the business.

(c) **Consistency concept**: A business should be consistent in its accounting treatment of similar items, both within a particular accounting period and between one accounting period and the next. This concept may not be applied if circumstances change including the introduction of a new accounting standard.

Example – the same rates of depreciation should be used from one period to the next unless there is a change of circumstances.

(d) **Duality**: Every transaction has two effects. The duality concept underpins double entry and the balance sheet, since every transaction affects two items in the balance sheet. Every time a transaction is recorded, both aspects must be taken into account.

Example – the payment of a telephone account requires an entry in the cash account and an equal and opposite entry in the telephone account.

(e) **Prudence:** According to the prudence concept, revenues and profits are not reported and recognised in the financial statements unless realised. Prudence requires that accounting policies take account of such uncertainty in recognising and measuring assets, liabilities, gains and losses.

Example – an item of stock whose net realisable value is less than its cost should be written down to its net realisable value in the balance sheet.

Answer 11

Turner (ACCA 12/98)

> ***Tutorial note:***
>
> This question tested competence at basic bookkeeping. Take care that you put the figures from the journal entries into the correct side of the suspense account.
>
> **Not required** - Narratives to the journal entries.

Suspense account

	£		£
Per TB	56,717	Sales returns (i)	8,980
Discount received (iii)	919	Purchase returns (i)	8,980
		Discount allowed (iii)	836
		Insurance (iv)	580
		Trial balance – telephone (v)	38,260
	57,636		57,636

Journal entries

		Dr £	*Cr* £
(i)	Sales returns	8,980	
	Suspense		8,980
	Purchases returns account	8,980	
	Suspense		8,980
(ii)	Plant cost	9,600	
	Plant repairs		9,600
	Profit and loss account	960	
	Plant provision for depreciation		960
(iii)	Discount allowed	836	
	Suspense		836
	Suspense	919	
	Discount received		919
(iv)	Insurance	580	
	Suspense		580
(v)	Trial balance – telephone	38,260	
	Suspense		38,260

(vi)	Sales	4,800	
	Motor vehicle disposals		4,800
	Motor vehicles disposals	12,000	
	Motor vehicles cost		12,000
	Motor vehicle depreciation	8,000	
	Motor vehicle disposals		8,000
	Motor vehicle disposals	800	
	Profit and loss account		800

Answer 12

Rook (ACCA 6/00)

Tutorial note:

This question required journal entries, with narratives, to record various transactions. Take care that you choose the correct side for the debit or credit.

Not required - Entries to ledger control accounts are not required for item (b).

		Dr £	*Cr* £
(a)	Salaries account	2,000	
	Suspense account		2,000
	Correction of understatement of debit side of salaries account in the nominal ledger.		
(b)	Motor vehicles account	6,000	
	Bad debts account	1,500	
	Wren Limited sales ledger account Acceptance of car in settlement of a sales ledger debt and the writing off of the balance of the debt to bad debts.		7,500
(c)	Factory account	46,100	
	Purchases account		27,600
	Wages account		18,500
	Materials and labour used in the construction of an extension to factory.		
(d)	Motor vehicles account	18,000	
	Plant and machinery account	33,000	
	Purchases account	20,000	
	Crow Limited loan account		71,000
	Purchase of assets from Crow Limited and establishing a loan account for the purchase price of the assets.		

(e)	(i)	Motor vehicles account	20,000	
		Car Dealer account		20,000
		Purchase of car on credit from Car Dealer.		
	(ii)	Disposal account	18,000	
		Motor vehicles account		18,000
		Cost of car given in part exchange to Car Dealer.		
	(iii)	Accumulated depreciation account	6,000	
		Disposal account		6,000
		Accumulated depreciation of car given in part exchange.		
	(iv)	Car Dealer account	12,000	
		Disposal account		12,000
		Part exchange value of car.		

Answer 13

MLN

> ***Tutorial note:***
>
> Questions on the reconciliation of the sales and purchases ledger are frequent in the examination and you should ensure that you are competent in this area.
>
> **Not required** - Explanations of your entries, other than narratives.

(a) *Suspense account*

		£			£
(1)	Sales ledger control	1,248		Per trial balance	2,045
(5)	Bank charges	66	(4)	Telephones	9
(7)	Fixed asset disposal	740			
		2,054			2,054

(b) *Sales ledger control account*

		£			£
	Balance brought down	327,762	(1)	Discount allowed	1,248
(2)	Sales	857	(3)	Contra	1,462
				Balance carried down	325,909
		328,619			328,619

Sales ledger listing

		£
	Balance per listing (balancing figure)	325,052
(2)	Debtor not included	857
	Adjusted listing (from control account)	325,909

(Note. Item (6) says ***purchase*** *not sales so ignore it.)*

(c)			£	£
	Net profit per draft accounts		412,967	
(2)	Add:	Credit sales to SEC Ltd	857	
				413,824
(4)	Less:	Telephone	9	
(6)		Purchases addition error	360	
(7)		Loss on disposal (740 – 800)	60	
				429
	Adjusted net profit			413,395

Answer 14

YTZ

(a) *Suspense account*

	£		£
Sales ledger control	3,200 (8)	Trial balance difference	
Cash – bank charges	23 (9)	(103,457 – 102,113)	1,344
		Travel expenses	9 (1)
		Purchase ledger control	1,870 (4)
	3,223		3,223

(b)

	£
Draft net profit	97,499
Travel expenses	(9) (1)
Returns outwards undercast	100 (2)
Electricity accrued expense	(154) (3)
Overdraft interest	(28) (5)
Machinery incorrectly charged to repairs	1,450 (6)
Depreciation on machinery (20% × 1,450)	(290) (6)
Discounts allowed	(30) (7)
Adjusted profit	98,538

Notes

The journal entries for each of the errors are as follows.

		£	£
(1)	Travel expenses	9	
	Suspense		9
(2)	Purchase ledger control	100	
	Returns outwards/purchases returns		100
(3)	Electricity	154	
	Accruals		154
(4)	Purchase ledger control	1,870	
	Suspense		1,870
(5)	Interest payable	28	
	Bank		28
(6)	Machinery cost	1,450	
	Machinery repairs		1,450
	Depreciation charge (20% × 1,450)	290	
	Provision for depreciation		290
(7)	Discount allowed	30	
	Sales ledger control		30
(8)	Suspense	3,200	
	Sales ledger control		3,200
(9)	Suspense	23	
	Bank		23

It is always recommended that you write out journals in full for each adjustment. This will make the statement of adjustment to profits much easier to do.

Answer 15

Provision (ACCA 12/93)

> ***Tutorial note:***
>
> The information provided in the question allows you to work out the debtors at the end of each year. These balances are then used to calculate the doubtful debts provision balance.

(a) *Provision for doubtful debts*

20X1		£	*20X1*		£
31.12	Sales ledger control a/c	600	01.01	Balance brought forward	1,000
31.12	Balance c/f (W2)	1,470	31.12	P&L a/c (balancing figure)	1,070
		2,070			2,070

20X2			20X2		
31.12	P&L a/c (balancing figure)	520	01.01	Balance brought forward	1,470
31.12	Balance c/f (W3)	950			
		1,470			1,470
			20X3		
			01.01	Balance brought forward	950

Workings

(W1) *Sales ledger control account*

20X1		£	20X1		£
01.01	Balance brought forward		31.12	Cash receipts	80,000
	(£1,000 × $\frac{100}{5}$)	20,000	31.12	Provision for doubtful debts	600
31.12	Sales	90,000	31.12	Balance c/f	29,400
		110,000			110,000
20X2			*20X2*		
01.01	Balance b/f	29,400	31.12	Cash receipts	110,000
31.12	Sales	100,000		Bad debts	400
			31.12	Balance c/f	19,000
		129,400			129,400

(W2) The closing balance on debtors is £29,400 (W1). Therefore the closing provision should be:

£29,400 × 5% = £1,470

(W3) The closing balance on debtors is £19,000 (W1). Therefore the closing provision should be:

£19,000 × 5% = £950

(b) The balance on the provision account is not a liability. It is a reduction in the asset (debtors) to account for the cost of debts that may not be collected.

Answer 16

Wholesalers

> ***Tutorial note:***
>
> The question states that the information in the question is unaudited. This should alert you to the possibility that there is an error – in this case in the sales day book.
>
> **Not required** - Full individual ledger accounts.

Sales ledger control account

	£		£
Opening balance	50,000	Sales returns	5,000
Sales	107,000	Cash book receipts	111,000
		Discounts allowed	3,000
		Bad debts	2,000
		Contra	6,000
		Closing balance	30,000
	157,000		157,000
Balance brought forward	30,000		

Provision for doubtful debts

	£		£
Closing balance (W1)	2,360	Opening balance	2,000
		Profit and loss account	360
	2,360		2,360
		Balance brought forward	2,360

		£
(W1)	Specific provision - C	1,000
	General provision 4% × (35,000 – 1,000)	1,360
		2,360

Note: In calculating the general provision, the credit balances on the debtors accounts are ignored.

	A £000	B £000	C £000	D £000	E £000	F £000	G £000	Totals £000
Opening balance	10	20	8	9	6	(2)	(1)	50
Sales	30	35		18	9	8	7	107
Sales returns	(2)					(3)		(5)
Cash receipts	(35)	(30)	(5)	(20)	(12)	(5)	(4)	(111)
Discounts allowed	(2)					(1)		(3)
Bad debts			(2)					(2)
Contra					(2)		(4)	(6)
	1	25	1	7	1	(3)	(2)	30

Note. Check all additions in questions if you are told that the figures are unreliable – here the sales day book additions were wrong!

Answer 17

Averill

Tutorial note:

The question concerned purchases and sales of fixed assets in the motor vehicles account.

Not required - Extracts of profit and loss account and balance sheet.

Motor vehicles at cost

		£			£
1 Oct 20X2	Balance b/d	10,000	24 Apr 20X3	Disposal (MV05)	4,000
31 Jan 20X3	Cash (MV11)	9,000	30 Sep 20X3	Balance c/d	15,000
		19,000			19,000
1 Oct 20X3	Balance b/d	15,000	31 Aug 20X4	Disposal (MV11)	9,000
20 Feb 20X4	Cash (MV12)	12,000	30 Sep 20X4	Balance c/d	32,000
31 Aug 20X4	Disposal – trade- in Cash (MV13)	7,400 6,600			
		41,000			41,000
1 Oct 20X4	Balance b/d	32,000			

Provision for depreciation of motor vehicles

		£			£
24 Apr 20X3	Disposal (W1)	2,312	1 Oct 20X2	Balance b/d	4,000
30 Sep 20X3	Balance c/d	5,016	30 Sep 20X3	Charge for year (W2)	3,328
		7,328			7,328
31 Aug 20X4	Disposal (W3)	2,250	1 Oct 20X3	Balance b/d	5,016
30 Sep 20X4	Balance c/d	10,074	30 Sep 20X4	Charge for year (W4)	7,308
		12,324			12,324
			1 Oct 20X4	Balance b/d	10,074

Disposal of motor vehicles

		£			£
24 Apr 20X3	Motor vehicle cost	4,000	24 Apr 20X3	Provision for depreciation (W1)	2,312
			24 Apr 20X3	Cash	500
			30 Sep 20X3	Loss to P&L account	1,188
		4,000			4,000
31 Aug 20X4	Motor vehicle cost	9,000	31 Aug 20X4	Provision for depreciation (W3)	2,250
30 Sep 20X4	Profit to P&L a/c	650	31 Aug 20X4	Trade-in allowance	7,400
		9,650			9,650

Workings

(W1) *MV05*

		£
30 September 20X0	£4,000 × 25%	1,000
30 September 20X1	£3,000 × 25%	750
30 September 20X2	£2,250 × 25%	562
		2,312

(W2) *30 September 20X3* *Depreciation charge*

Policy is 25% on net book value.

Net book value	=	Cost – accumulated depreciation
	=	£15,000 – (4,000 – 2,312)
	=	£13,312
Depreciation	=	£3,328

(W3) *MV 11 accumulated depreciation up until disposal*

One year 25% on net book value.

£9,000 × 25% = £2,250

(W4) *30 September 20X4* *Depreciation charge*

Same policy as before.

Net book value	=	£32,000 – (£5,016 - £2,250)
Net book value	=	£29,234
Depreciation	=	£7,308

Answer 18

Diamond (ACCA 6/97)

Freehold land – cost or valuation

20X5		*£000*	*20X5*		*£000*
01 Jan	Balance b/d	1,000	31 Dec	Balance c/d	1,000
		1,000			1,000
20X6					
01 Jan	Balance b/d	1,000			
31 Dec	Revaluation reserve	200	31 Dec	Balance c/d	1,200
		1,200			1,200
20X7					
01 Jan	Balance b/d	1,200			

Freehold buildings - cost

20X5		£000	20X5		£000
01 Jan	Balance b/d	500			
08 Oct	Cash	50	31 Dec	Balance c/d	550
		550			550
20X6					
01 Jan	Balance b/d	550			

Freehold building – provision for depreciation

20X5		£000	20X5		£000
			01 Jan	Balance b/d	210
31 Dec	Balance c/d	221	31 Dec	Profit and loss	11
		221			221
20X6			20X6		
			01 Jan	Balance b/d	221
31 Dec	Balance c/d	232	31 Dec	Profit and loss	11
		232			232
			20X7		
			01 Jan	Balance b/d	232

Office equipment - cost

20X5		£000	20X5		£000
01 Jan	Balance b/d	40	10 June	Disposal	8
10 June	Cash	12	31 Dec	Balance c/d	48
	Disposal	4			
		56			56
20X6			20X6		
01 Jan	Balance b/d	48	01 Mar	Disposal	8
			31 Dec	Balance c/d	40
		48			48
20X7					
01 Jan	Balance b/d	40			

Office equipment – provision for depreciation

20X5		*£000*	*20X5*		*£000*
10 June	Disposal	7	01 Jan	Balance b/d	24
31 Dec	Balance c/d	23	31 Dec	Profit and loss	6
		30			30
20X6			*20X6*		
01 Mar	Disposal	6	01 Jan	Balance b/d	23
31 Dec	Balance c/d	22	31 Dec	Profit and loss	5
		28			28
			20X7		
			01 Jan	Balance b/d	22

Office equipment - disposal

20X5		*£000*	*20X5*		*£000*
10 June	Equipment cost	8	10 June	Office equip dep'n	7
31 Dec	Profit and loss – profit	3		Office equip – cost	4
		11			11
20X6			*20X6*		
01 Mar	Office equip cost	8	01 Mar	Office equip dep'n	6
31 Dec	Profit and loss – profit	1		Cash – proceeds of sale	3
		9			9

Answer 19

FRS 15

Tutorial note:

This question relates to cost, expected life and residual value as the factors determining depreciation.

Not required - Methods of depreciation.

FRS 15 employs depreciation as a method of spreading the cost of a tangible fixed asset over its estimated useful life, ie the period over which the asset will generate additional income for the business.

Assume an item of plant cost £4,000 and that it has a nil scrap value at the end of five years. Since expenditure on the asset will benefit the revenues of the next five years, the accruals (or matching) concept requires us to match the £4,000 cost against all of those revenues. The profit and loss account for each of those years (in this case five) is charged with part of the cost of the asset.

Factors that affect the amount of depreciation charged include the following.

- The useful life of the asset. The shorter the life the more depreciation will need to be charged each year. For example, plant and machinery of a specialised nature can quickly become obsolete and will need to be replaced by updated versions.
- The type of asset. For example, motor vehicles might be used most in the early years of their life and so more depreciation should be charged in these early years.
- The residual value of the asset. The higher the residual value of the asset, the lower the amount of depreciation that will need to be charged each year. This is since a lower proportion of the cost of the asset is being consumed by the business over the useful life.

Answer 20

Stoat (ACCA 12/99)

MEMORANDUM

To: Directors of Stoat Limited
From: A N Accountant
Date: X-X-XX

Depreciation and fixed asset valuation

(a) Evidence to check whether the company's depreciation rates are likely to be too low:

  (i) Proceeds from sales of fixed assets being substantially lower than their net book value at date of sale giving rise to losses on sale.

  (ii) Comparisons with trade journals, associations and other companies' financial statements.

  (iii) Reviews by external bodies, eg the auditors.

(b) Disclosures required on change of depreciation methods.

A change from one method of providing depreciation to another is permissible only on the grounds that the new method will give a fairer presentation.

  (i) The effect of the change on the financial statements for that year, if material.

  (ii) The reason for the change.

(c) The requirements regarding revaluation of fixed assets.

  (i) Classes of assets should be similarly treated in that if any asset of a class is revalued, all assets of that class must be revalued.

  (ii) Valuations must be kept up-to-date.

  (iii) Disclosure of the name and qualification of the valuer, the basis of valuation and the date and amounts of valuations.

Answer 21

Pentland (ACCA 12/00)

> ***Tutorial note:***
>
> This question required the ledger accounts to record various fixed asset transactions. Each class of asset should have separate cost, accumulated depreciation and disposal accounts.

Buildings – cost or valuation

		£000			£000
20X0			*20X1*		
01 July	Balance b/f	2,200	30 June	Balance c/f	3,400
20X1					
01 Jan	Revaluation	1,200			
		3,400			3,400
20X1					
1 July	Balance b/f	3,400			

Revaluation reserve

		£000			£000
20X1			*20X1*		
30 June	Balance c/f	2,022	01 Jan	Buildings – cost/ valuation	1,200
			01 Jan	Buildings – accum depreciation	822
		2,022			2,022
			20X1		
			01 July	Balance b/f	2,022

Buildings – accumulated depreciation

	£000		£000
Revaluation	822	Balance b/f	800
		Profit and loss account – depreciation to 31 Dec 20X0 2% × £2,200,000 × 6/12	22
Balance c/f	34	Profit and loss account – depreciation to 30 June 20X1 2% × £3,400,000 × 6/12	34
	34		34
		Balance b/f	34

Motor vehicles - cost

20X0		*£000*	*20X1*		*£000*
01 July	Balance b/f	600	01 April	Motor vehicles – disposal	20
20X1					
01 April	Cash	18			
	Motor vehicles – disposal	12	30 June	Balance c/f	610
		630			630

Motor vehicles – accumulated depreciation

20X1		*£000*	*20X0*		*£000*
01 April	Motor vehicles – disposal	13	01 July	Balance b/f	200
	(£10,000 + £3,000 (W2)		*20X1*		
30 June	Balance c/f	307.5	30 June	Profit and loss a/c (W1)	120.5
		320.5			320.5

Motor vehicles - disposal

20X1		*£000*	*20X1*		*£000*
01 April	Motor vehicle cost	20	01 April	Motor vehicle cost - agreed value	12
30 June	Profit and loss account			Motor vehicles -	
	Profit on sale	5		accum depreciation	13
		25			25

Working

Motor vehicles – depreciation

		£000
Vehicle given in part exchange	20% × £20,000 × 9/12	3
Remaining vehicles	20% × £580,000	116
New vehicles	20% × £30,000 × 3/12	1.5
		120.5

Answer 22

Cost and NRV

> ***Tutorial note:***
>
> This question refers to well known conventions that you must be able to explain.
>
> **Not required** - Other methods of stock valuation.

(a) (i) *Historical cost* is the original cost to the business of assets and expenses.

(ii) *Net realisable value* is the expected sale value of the asset in the ordinary course of business, less any costs to completion and any costs of realisation.

(iii) The *prudence convention* is the convention that accountants should only recognise revenues when they are reasonably certain that they will arise but that they should recognise expenses or liabilities as soon as they are known. Generally this will mean that accountants will tend to be pessimistic in their preparation of financial statements and understate assets and net profits.

(iv) The *consistency convention* is that financial statements should be prepared from one year to the next in such a way that they are comparable. Therefore similar items should be treated in the same way in the financial statements within each period and from year to year.

(b) It could be argued that the quotation is correct. Under this policy the same type of stock item may be valued in different ways in different years. However, what is really being applied is a consistent policy of prudence, therefore one can also argue that there is indeed consistency of treatment.

(c) The main argument in favour of this policy is the argument of prudence. Users of the financial statements can be assured that the figure for stock has not been over-estimated given the nature of the stock itself and the type of business. Therefore loan creditors can be assured that the value for stock in the balance sheet is at least what the stock will actually realise and shareholders can be confident that any losses due to the condition of the items of stock have already been taken into account.

Under the prudence policy there is a deliberate tendency towards understating assets and profits and this is unlikely to help in providing an accurate picture of the business. Also as argued in part (b) above there is an element of inconsistency in this policy and perhaps it would be better either to value all stock at cost, regardless of future realisation value, or to value stocks at their total realisable value rather than a mixture of the two.

Answer 23

SSAP 9 (ACCA 6/98)

> ***Tutorial note:***
>
> This is a question on stock, in accordance with SSAP 9. A manufacturer's costs are labour, materials and overheads as explained in SSAP 9 *Stocks and Long-term Contracts.*
>
> **Not required** - Discussions outside of SSAP 9.

(a) **LIFO**

Last in, first out. This means that stock is used or sold on the basis that the last goods in stock are the first goods sent out. The closing stock balance is then made up of the goods purchased first at the price that they were purchased at.

(b) **Acceptable methods**

Unit cost

This is a simple method if units can be easily identified separately. Each unit is valued at the price at which it was purchased. This represents the actual cost of the stock.

First in, first out (FIFO)

Stock is used or sold on the basis that the first goods in will be the first goods out and so closing stock is based on the most recently purchased goods at the most current price. This means that the value of the stock is a more current value.

Average cost (AVCO)

Stock is based on the weighted average price of all stock purchased in the period. The balance will roll forward at the end of each period. This is a good approximation of the cost of the goods making up the stock held.

LIFO is not acceptable under SSAP 9 as it will not normally give a good approximation of the actual cost of the goods held in stock.

(c) Stock in a manufacturing business would be arrived at by using not only the cost of the materials consumed, but the cost of labour and any appropriate overheads. These would be allocated based on the normal level of production and should include all selling and administration expenses.

Answer 24

Sampi (ACCA 6/98)

(a) **LIFO**

	Opening stock units	Deliveries from factory 8 March units	Deliveries from factory 22 March units
	4,000		
Sales		3,800	
12 March	(1,200)	(3,800)	
	2,800	-	
18 March	(2,000)		
	800		
			6,000
24 March			(3,000)
			3,000
28 March			(2,000)
			1,000
Closing stock			
800 at £12	9,600		
1,000 at £18	18,000		
	27,600		

(b) **Value of stock using weighted average basis**

	Number of units	Weighted average cost £	Total value of closing stock £
Opening stock	4,000	13.00	
8 March	3,800	15.00	
Balance	7,800	13.97	
12 March	(5,000)		
	2,800	13.97	
18 March	(2,000)		
	800	13.97	

22 March	6,000	18.00	
	6,800	17.53	
24 March	(3,000)		
	3,800	17.53	
28 March	(2,000)		
	1,800	17.53	31,554

Answer 25

Journals

> ***Tutorial note:***
>
> This question tests basic competence of journal entries.
>
> **Not required** - Narrative descriptions to the journals.

		Dr £	*Cr* £
(a)	Sales	180	
	Debtors control		180
	Debtors ledger		180
(b)	Debtors ledger	800	
(c)	Discounts allowed	70	
	Debtors control		70
	Debtors ledger		70
(d)	Sales	198	
	Debtors control		198
	Debtors ledger		198
(e)	Creditors control	600	
	Debtors control		600
	Creditors ledger	600	
	Debtors ledger		600
(f)	Debtors ledger		160

Answer 26

Scimitar (ACCA 12/97)

> ***Tutorial note:***
>
> This is a control account reconciliation. Take care that you enter the figures on the correct side of the control accounts.

Sales ledger control account

20X7		£	*20X7*		£
01 Sep	Balance b/d	188,360	01 Sep	Balance b/d	2,140
30 Sep	Sales		30 Sep	Sales returns	9,160
	(101,260 + 1,360) (ii)	102,620		Cash received	91,270
	Cash refunds	300		Cash discounts	1,430
	Petty cash refund (iv)	20		Bad debts written off	460
	Balance c/d (W1)	3,320		Contras (480 + 500)	980
				Balance c/d	189,180
		294,620			294,620

Purchases ledger control account

20X7		£	*20X7*		£
01 Sep	Balance b/d	120	01 Sep	Balance b/d	89,410
30 Sep	Purchases returns	4,280	30 Sep	Purchases	
				(68,420 – 1,360) (iii)	67,060
	Cash to suppliers	71,840		Balance carried down	90
	Cash discounts	880			
	Contras	980			
	Balance carried down	78,460			
		156,560			156,560

(W1) *Sales ledger credit balances*

	£
Draft closing balance	2,680
Omitted balance (i)	680
Wrong way adjustment of £20 refund	(40)
	3,320

Answer 27

Theta (ACCA 6/98)

> ***Tutorial note:***
>
> You should assume that narrations are required for journal entries unless told to the contrary.
>
> Note that the credit balances in the sales ledger should be added to creditors, not deducted from debtors.

(a) **Journals**

		Dr £	*Cr* £
(i)	Zeta Ltd purchase ledger	1,080	
	Zeta Ltd sales ledger		1,080
	(Being contra settlement)		
(ii)	Bad debts	3,590	
	P		840
	Q		120
	R		360
	S		2,090
	T		180
	(Being bad debts written off)		
(iii)	Profit and loss account (5,200 – 3,060)	2,140	
	Provision for doubtful debts		2,140
	(Being an increase in the provision for doubtful debts)		
(iv)	Vau Ltd sales ledger	200	
	Tau Ltd sales ledger		200
	(Being correction of misposted cash receipt)		

(b) *Debtors*

	£
Sales ledger balance	384,600
Contra settlement (i)	(1,080)
Bad debt write offs (ii)	(3,590)
	379,930
Less Provision for doubtful debts	(5,200)
Debtors	374,730
Purchase ledger debit balances	1,860
	376,590

Creditors: amounts falling due within one year		
Purchase ledger balance		222,230
Contra settlement (i)		(1,080)
		221,150
Less	Long-term creditors	(28,000)
Creditors		193,150
Sales ledger credit balances		2,900
		196,050
Creditors: amounts falling due after more than one year		28,000

Answer 28

Computer systems

> ***Tutorial note:***
>
> This question concerned computerised and manual accounting systems.

(a) Choose two from the following:

- *Extraction error*

  Error in compiling the total of the sales ledger balance. Either omission, transposition or extracting debits as credits or *vice versa.*

- *Addition errors*

  Error in calculating the balances on accounts.

- *Posting errors*

  Errors in transferring entries from one record to another.

(b) Choose two from the following:

- *Omission*

  A complete transaction is missed out of the records. This could happen in either system where controls are insufficient.

- *Transaction recorded incorrectly*

  In a manual system an invoice could be incorrectly recorded in the day book. In the computer system it could be keyed in incorrectly.

- *Transaction recorded at an incorrect account*

  Human error can always give rise to mispostings whether in a manual or computerised system, unless controls are put in place.

Answer 29

Computerised accounting systems

Advantages of computerised systems:

- *Accuracy*

  Problems such as calculation errors will be eliminated and this will improve the accuracy of information.

- *Speed*

  Large amounts of data can be processed at considerably greater speeds than in a manual system.

- *Cost*

  The cost of processing data may be reduced.

- *Storage*

  A large volume of information can be stored and retrieved easily using various computer storage devices.

Disadvantages of computerised systems:

- *Set-up costs*

  Whenever a new computer system is implemented, it will result in high costs relating to both hardware and software.

- *Inflexibility*

  A manual system can be revised with relative ease whereas a computer system is often more difficult and costly to update.

- *Dependence*

  Once a system is in place, high volumes of data will be processed by a small team. However, if the system breaks down it can have serious implications.

Answer 30

Andy (ACCA 6/99 adapted)

> ***Tutorial note:***
>
> This question is on basic bookkeeping and should provide reasonably easy marks.

(a) *Andy – cash book*

	£		£
Balance b/f	9,780	Bank charges (3)	640
Correction of error – interest	640	Plant (4)	20,000
Balance c/f	23,780	Dishonoured cheque (5)	1,960
		Misposted payment (6)	9,600
		Error in addition (7)	2,000
	34,200		34,200

(b) **Statement as at 31 March 20X9**

	£
Balance per bank statement (balancing figure)	(25,600)
Lodgements not credited (2)	5,780
	(19,820)
Dishonoured cheque	(1,960)
Outstanding cheque (1)	(2,000)
Balance per cash book	(23,780)

(c) **Statement of effect on profit**

	£ +	£ -	£
Profit per draft accounts			162,416
Bank charges (3)		640	
Depreciation (4)		2,000	
Bad debt (5)		1,960	
Motor expenses (6)		4,800	
Additional depreciation (6)		1,200	
Purchases understated (7)		2,000	
Interest adjustment (8)	640		
Repairs to premises (9)	1,740		
	2,380	12,600	
			(10,220)
Adjusted profit			152,196

Answer 31

Otter (ACCA 12/99)

> ***Tutorial note:***
>
> This question required the preparation of control accounts for sales and purchases.
>
> **Not required** - Mention of underlying ledgers – the question states that these have been agreed to the control accounts.

Sales ledger – control account

	£		£
Opening balances b/f	386,430	Opening balances b/f	190
Sales (163,194 + 1,386) (1)	164,580	Cash received	158,288
Cash refund (2)	350	Discounts allowed	2,160
		Returns inwards	590
		Contra (3)	870
		Bad debts written off (4)	1,360
Closing balances c/f	370	Closing balances c/f	388,272
	551,730		551,730

Purchase ledger control account

	£		£
Opening balances b/f	520	Opening balances b/f	184,740
Cash paid (103,040 – 350) (2)	102,690	Purchases (98,192 + 1,395 – 1,359) (6)	98,228
Discounts received	990	Bad debt written off (8)	420
Returns outwards (1,370 +2,000) (5)	3,370		
Contra (3)	870		
Closing balances c/f	175,048	Closing balances c/f (520 – 420) (8)	100
	283,488		283,488

Note that adjustment (7) does not appear in the purchase ledger control account. It only affects the individual accounts.

The references in brackets refer to the errors and adjustments listed in the question.

Answer 32

Halberd (ACCA 12/97 adapted)

> ***Tutorial note:***
>
> This is a fairly straightforward incomplete records question. You will need to construct a debtors control account to calculate the figure for sales for the year.
>
> **Not required** - VAT is specifically excluded by the question.

HALBERD - TRADING AND PROFIT AND LOSS ACCOUNT FOR THE YEAR ENDED 30 JUNE 20X4

	£	£
Sales (W1)		154,610
Cost of sales		
Opening stock	680	
Purchases (81,470 – 400)	81,070	
	81,750	
Closing stock	(810)	
		(80,940)
Gross profit		73,670
Expenses:		
Staff wages	21,400	
Rent and rates (8,600 + 850 – 1,000)	8,450	
Insurance (1,400 + 300 – 350)	1,350	
Van expenses (3,270 – 320)	2,950	
Miscellaneous expenses (3,600 + 200 – 120)	3,680	
Depreciation:		
Refrigeration equipment (10% × 8,400)	840	
Shop fittings (15% × (3,720 + 1,570 – 2,090))	480	
Van (25% × 9,200)	2,300	
Bad and doubtful debts	1,860	
Interest on loan	500	
		(43,810)
Net profit		29,860

Workings

(W1) *Credit sales*

Sales ledger control account

	£		£
Opening balance	4,270	Credit customer receipts	28,440
Sales on credit (balancing figure)	30,360	Closing balance	6,190
	34,630		34,630

(W2) *Sales*

	£
Cash sales	108,600
Credit sales	30,360
Re drawings	15,600
Cash balance increase	50
	154,610

Answer 33

Ernie (ACCA 12/98)

> ***Tutorial note:***
>
> Note to adjust cash receipts and payments by opening and closing balances, refunds and bad debts to arrive at sales and purchases.
>
> **Not required** - Full T accounts for all expense accounts.

TRADING AND PROFIT AND LOSS ACCOUNT
FOR THE YEAR ENDED 30 JUNE 20X8

	£	£
Sales (W1)		204,490
Cost of sales:		
Opening stock	14,160	
Purchases (W2)	84,620	
Wages of repair staff	68,200	
	166,980	
Less: Closing stock	(12,170)	
		(154,810)
Gross profit		49,680

Expenses:			
Salaries		5,000	
Rent	(3,600 + 750 – 900)	3,450	
Telephone	(860 + 240 – 210)	890	
Electricity	(890 + 220 – 180)	930	
Insurance	(700 + 800)	1,500	
Miscellaneous expenses	(1,280 + 490)	1,770	
Bad debts		1,280	
Depreciation on plant	(25% × (12,600 + 8,400 – 5,800))	3,800	
Depreciation on motor van	(½ × 25% × 12,800)	1,600	
Profit on sale of van (W3)		(500)	
Loan interest	(10% × 10,000) × 3/12	250	
			(19,970)
Net profit for year to date			29,710

Workings

(W1) *Debtors*

	£		£
Balance b/f	9,490	Cash from customers	52,640
			150,880
Refund to customer	400	Bad debts	1,280
Sales (balancing figure)	204,490	Balance c/f (10,860 – 1,280)	9,580
	214,380		214,380

(W2) *Creditors*

	£		£
Cash to suppliers	83,990	Balance b/f	3,460
Balance c/f	4,090	Purchases (balancing figure)	84,620
	88,080		88,080

(W3) *Disposals*

	£		£
Cost	9,000	Depreciation	6,500
Profit on sale	500	Proceeds	3,000
	9,500		9,500

Answer 34

Goshawk (ACCA 6/00)

> ***Tutorial note:***
>
> This question required the preparation of a trading and profit and loss account for a sole trader.

(a) *GOSHAWK*
TRADING AND PROFIT AND LOSS ACCOUNT
FOR THE YEAR ENDED 31 MARCH 20X2

		£	£
Sales revenue (W1)			300,000
Less:	Cost of sales		
	Opening stock	28,500	
	Purchases (W2)	220,830	
		249,330	
Less:	Closing stock	37,100	
			212,230
Gross profit			87,770
Less:	Expenses		
	Staff wages	25,870	
	Insurance (800 + 2,000 – 1,000)	1,800	
	Miscellaneous expenses (2,180 + 1,300 + 2,100 – 1,800)	3,780	
	Amortisation of lease (W3)	5,000	
	Depreciation of shop fittings (W4)	5,460	
	Loan interest	10,000	
			51,910
Net profit			35,860

Workings

(W1) *Debtors*

	£		£
Opening debtors b/f	1,380	Cash received	300,880
Refunds to customers	960	(299,580 + 1,300)	
Sales (balancing figure)	300,000	Closing debtors c/f	1,460
	302,340		302,340

(W2) *Creditors*

	£		£
Cash paid	211,830	Opening creditors b/f	39,000
Closing creditors c/f	48,000	Purchases (balancing figure)	220,830
	259,830		259,830

(W3) *Amortisation of lease*

$$\frac{£200{,}000}{40} = £5{,}000$$

(W4) *Depreciation of shop fittings*

Cost at 01/04/X0	£28,000
Depreciation @ 15%	£4,200
Cost at 01/04/X1	£28,000
Additions in year	£8,400
	£36,400
Depreciation @ 15%	£5,460

(b) **Possible cost of the items of stock stolen**

Sales £	*Mark-up on cost*	*Gross profit* £
252,000	Balancing figure 50% ($\times \frac{50}{150}$) =	84,000
14,000	Security uniforms 40% ($\times \frac{40}{140}$) =	4,000
34,000	Reduced mark-up 25% ($\times \frac{25}{125}$) =	6,800
300,000	Expected gross profit	94,800
	Actual gross profit	87,770
	Possible cost of stock stolen	7,030

Answer 35

Zed (ACCA 6/94)

> ***Tutorial note:***
>
> This is a reasonably straightforward incomplete records problem.
>
> **Not required** - Compliance with Companies Act disclosure requirements.

BALANCE SHEET AS AT 31 DECEMBER 20X3

	Cost *£000*	*Depreciation* *£000*	*£000*
Fixed assets			
Land			130
Building	80	6	74
Machinery	90	52	38
			242
Current assets			
Stock		40	
Debtors		35	
Bank (W3)		56	
		131	
Current liabilities			
Creditors (25 + 10)		35	
Net current assets			96
Debentures			(50)
			288
Capital and reserves			
Ordinary shares of £1 each			130
Preference shares of £1 each			40
Share premium			30
Revaluation reserve			50
Profit and loss (34 + 4) (W4)			38
			288

Workings

(W1) *Debtors ledger control*

	£000		£000
Opening balance	24	Closing balance	35
Sales	920	Bad debts	5
		Contra	8
		Cash received (balancing figure)	896
	944		944

(W2) *Creditors ledger control*

	£000		£000
Closing balance	25	Opening balance	28
Contra	8	Purchases	500
Cash paid (balancing figure)	495		
	528		528

(W3) *Bank control*

	£000		£000
Debtors ledger control (W1)	896	Opening balance	7
Share issue	60	Creditors ledger control (W2)	495
		Operating expenses paid	360
		Debenture interest	8
		Preference dividends	4
		Ordinary dividends	26
		Closing balance (balancing figure)	56
	956		956

(W4)

	£000
Sales	920
Cost of sales (35 + 500 – 40)	(495)
Operating expenses (360 + 10 – 2)	(368)
Depreciation (9 + 1)	(10)
Bad debt	(5)
Interest	(8)
Dividends	(30)
Retained profit	4

Answer 36

Provisions

A provision is an amount set aside to provide for a liability, loss or fall in value of an asset which is either likely to occur, or certain to occur but where the amount is uncertain, eg depreciation, or a provision made for a possible legal claim for damages for breach of contract.

Any balances in a company balance sheet representing profits or surpluses, whether they are realised or not, are collectively referred to as reserves. A reserve forms part of the ownership interest of a company. A reserve can be made up of:

- surpluses above the nominal value of share capital (share premium)
- accumulated profits
- revaluation of fixed assets.

The main distinction is that a provision represents a liability or potential loss, whereas a reserve represents owner's equity.

Answer 37

Grace

> ***Tutorial note:***
>
> Note that the question asks for a profit and loss account 'for internal purposes'.
>
> **Not required** - Notes to the accounts.

PROFIT AND LOSS ACCOUNT FOR THE YEAR ENDED 31 DECEMBER 20X7

	£000	*£000*	*£000*
Sales, less returns inwards (750 – 3)			747
Cost of sales:			
Opening stock		200	
Purchases, less returns outwards (350 – 1)		349	
Carriage inwards		1	
		550	
Closing stock		(180)	
			370
Gross profit			377
General expenses (200 – 1 – 2)		197	
Advertising		10	
Carriage outwards		1	
Discounts allowed		3	
Discounts received		(1)	

Bad and doubtful debts (see working)		23	
Accountancy charges		1	
Depreciation: Vehicles	20		
Machinery	10		
		30	
Interest on debentures (100 × 10%)		10	
			(274)
Net profit			103
Proposed dividend (200,000 × 0.05)			(10)
			93
Profit and loss account balance brought forward			100
Profit and loss account balance carried forward			193

Workings

Bad and doubtful debts

The trick here is to remember to deduct the bad debt before calculating the 5% provision.

	£000
Debtors per trial balance	200
Less: Bad debt written off	20
	180
Provision required £180,000 at 5%	9
Provision already in existence	6
Increase in provision	3
Bad debt written off	20
Charge to profit and loss account	23

Tutorial notes

(i) Details of the discounts, returns and carriage need to be calculated with care. In the case of discounts and returns, the two figures are 'opposites' (one debit and one credit) and the missing figures have to be calculated by *adding* the given figure to the balance provided. In the case of carriage, both carriage outwards and carriage inwards are expenses, and the figure for carriage inwards had to be found by *subtraction* - an ingenious device from the examiner here. Note that carriage inwards must be treated as a trading account item because it is part of the cost of purchases, while carriage outwards is a profit and loss account item because it is a service to customers.

Note too that discounts allowed and discounts received should be shown separately as in the answer above. If they are netted off an important change or trend in the figures may be obscured.

(ii) Questions of this kind often omit a direct requirement to provide for debenture interest, and leave the candidate to note that the debentures carry interest at 10% and thus only half a year's payment has yet been made. Be on the alert for such implied adjustments.

Answer 38

Arbalest (ACCA 12/97)

> ***Tutorial note:***
>
> In this question, you are given the opening balance sheet and an extract of the transactions in the year. You are required to consider only two notes.
>
> **Not required** - Closing balance sheet or ledger accounts for the transactions.

(a) **Movements on reserves**

	Share premium £000	*Revaluation reserve £000*	*Retained earnings £000*	*Total £000*
At 30 September 20X6	400		4,060	4,460
Rights issue	1,000			1,000
Bonus issue	(1,400)		(600)	(2,000)
Revaluation of assets		500		500
Retained profit for year			370	370
At 30 September 20X7	Nil	500	3,830	4,330

(b) **Movements on fixed assets**

	Land £000	*Buildings £000*	*Plant and machinery £000*	*Total £000*
Cost				
At 30 September 20X6	2,000	1,500	2,800	6,300
Additions	600	2,400	1,600	4,600
Disposals			(1,000)	(1,000)
Revaluation	500			500
At 30 September 20X7	3,100	3,900	3,400	10,400
Depreciation				
At 30 September 20X6	Nil	450	1,000	1,450
Charge for year	Nil	46 (W1)	220 (W2)	266
Disposals			(800)	(800)
At 30 September 20X7	Nil	496	420	916
Net book value 30 September 20X7	3,100	3,404	2,980	9,484
Net book value 30 September 20X6	2,000	1,050	1,800	4,850

Workings

(W1) Buildings depreciation charge

	£000
£1,500,000 × 2%	30
£2,400,000 × 2% × $\frac{4}{12}$	16
	46

(W2) Plant and machinery depreciation charge

	£000
£1,800,000 × 10%	180
£1,600,000 × 10% × $\frac{3}{12}$	40
	220

Answer 39

Koppa Ltd (ACCA 6/98)

> ***Tutorial note:***
>
> Note that this question requires statements 'in a form suitable for publication'. You must use a standard format.
>
> **Not required** - Notes other than reserve movements for the year.

BALANCE SHEET AS AT 31 DECEMBER 20X7

	£000	£000
Fixed assets		
Intangible assets		
Development costs (W1)		219
Tangible assets		
Land and buildings (2,200 + 900 – 100 – 18)		2,982
Office equipment (260 – 60 – 40)		160
Motor vehicles (200 – 90 – 50)		60
		3,421
Current assets		
Stock	880	
Debtors	1,360	
Prepayments	40	
Cash	90	
	2,370	

Creditors: amounts falling due within one year		
Trade creditors	820	
Accruals	15	
Proposed dividend (2,000 × 0.2)	400	
	1,235	
Net current assets		1,135
Total assets less current liabilities		4,556
Creditors: amounts falling due after more than one year		
12% debentures		(1,000)
		3,556
Capital and reserves		
Called up share capital		1,000
Share premium account		500
Revaluation reserve		200
Profit and loss account (1,272 + 584 (β))		1,856
		3,556

Movement on reserves

	Share premium £000	*Revaluation reserve £000*	*Profit and loss account £000*	*Total £000*
As at 31 December 20X6	-	-	1,272	1,272
Share issue	500			500
Revaluation of land		200		200
Retained profit for year			584	584
As at 31 December 20X7	500	200	1,856	2,556

Workings

(W1) *Capitalised development costs*

	£000
As at 1 January 20X7	180
New expenditure in year	59
	239
Amortised in year	(20)
As at 31 December 20X7	219

Answer 40

Topaz (ACCA 6/97)

> ***Tutorial note:***
>
> This question tests knowledge of the FRS 3 profit and loss account. Bear in mind the additional requirements of FRS 3: the separate presentation of continuing and discontinued activities, and the disclosure of exceptional items on the face of the profit and loss account or in a note as appropriate.
>
> **Not required** - Discussion of the required format other than as it relates to the information given.

(a) *TOPAZ LIMITED*
PROFIT AND LOSS ACCOUNT FOR THE YEAR ENDED 31 DECEMBER 20X6

	Continuing operations *£m*	*Discontinued operations* *£m*	*Total* *£m*
Sales	68.0	13.0	81.0
Cost of sales	(41.0)	(8.0)	(49.0)
Gross profit	27.0	5	32.0
Distribution costs (*Note*)	(6.0)	(1.0)	(7.0)
Administrative expenses	(4.0)	(2.0)	(6.0)
Operating profit	17.0	2.0	19.0
Profit on sale of discontinued operations		2.5	2.5
Costs of fundamental reorganisation	(1.8)		(1.8)
Profit on ordinary activities before interest	15.2	4.5	19.7
Interest payable			(1.0)
Profit on ordinary activities before taxation			18.7
Taxation			(4.8)
Profit on ordinary activities after taxation			13.9
Dividends			
Interim paid			(2.0)
Final proposed			(4.0)
Retained profit for the financial year			7.9

Note. The bad debt of £1.9 million is an exceptional item but it is included in distribution costs as it does not require separate disclosure.

(b) *TOPAZ LIMITED*
STATEMENT OF TOTAL RECOGNISED GAINS AND LOSSES

	£m
Profit for the financial year	13.9
Unrealised surplus on revaluation of properties	4.0
Total gains recognised since last annual report	17.9

Answer 41

FRS 3 (ACCA 12/98)

> ***Tutorial note:***
>
> Note that the only area of the FRS 3 presentation that you need to discuss is discontinued operations and acquisitions. Make sure that you also discuss the advantages to users.
>
> **Not required** - A general discussion of FRS 3.

(a) FRS 3 requires that the profit and loss account should be analysed between continuing operations and discontinued operations from sales to operating profit.

Within continuing operations there should be a further analysis between new acquisitions in the year and existing business.

Any profit or loss on disposal of discontinuing operations should be disclosed separately on the face of the profit and loss account.

Advantages of the requirements.

(i) Such analysis will assist the user in understanding the events which have contributed to the performance for the period.

(ii) Disclosing the profit or loss on disposal of a discontinued operation separately will remove any distortions to operating profit.

(iii) Splitting out new acquisitions from existing business allows a more accurate comparison to be made from one year to the next.

(iv) Disclosing discontinued activities separately allows forecasts to be made on continuing activities alone, ie sales and profits.

It also allows the potential investor to see the profits which will generate future dividends.

(b) Three items which appear in the statement of total recognised gains and losses.

(i) Unrealised surplus on revaluation of fixed assets.

(ii) Profit before dividends.

(iii) Prior year adjustments.

Answer 42

Leonardo (ACCA 12/98)

> ***Tutorial note:***
>
> Note that marks are specifically awarded for layout.

PROFIT AND LOSS ACCOUNT FOR THE YEAR ENDED 30 SEPTEMBER 20X8

	£000
Sales	6,840
Cost of sales (W)	(3,988)
Gross profit	2,852
Distribution costs (880 + 50 + 400)	(1,330)
Administrative expenses	(590)
Operating profit	932
Cost of fundamental reorganisation	(560)
Profit on sale of property	1,200
Profit on ordinary activities before interest	1,572
Interest payable	(300)
Profit on ordinary activities before taxation	1,272
Tax on profit on ordinary activities	(300)
Profit for the financial year	972

Note. Operating profit £932,000 is calculated after charging an exceptionally large bad debt of £400,000 which has been written off.

Working: cost of sales

	£000
Opening stock	1,200
Purchases	3,670
	4,870
Less: Closing stock (950 – 68)	(882)
	3,988

Answer 43

Atok (ACCA 12/99)

> ***Tutorial note:***
>
> This question requires the preparation of a company's profit and loss account.
>
> **Not required** - Notes to the statements other than reserve movements.

(a) *ATOK LIMITED*
PROFIT AND LOSS ACCOUNT FOR THE YEAR ENDED 30 JUNE 20X1

	£000
Sales revenue (14,800 – 24 (1))	14,776
Cost of sales (W1)	(10,280)
Gross profit	4,496
Distribution costs (1,080 + 190 – 120 + 272) (W2)	(1,422)
Administrative expenses (1,460 + 70 – 60 + 272) (W2)	(1,742)
Operating profit	1,332
Interest payable ($\frac{3}{12} \times 10\% \times £2,000,000$)	(50)
Profit for the financial year	1,282
Proposed dividend (10,000 + 4,000) × 2 × £0.025	(700)
Retained profit	582

(b) **Statement of movements in reserves**

	Share premium account £000	*Revaluation reserve £000*	*Profit and loss account £000*	*Total £000*
As at 1 July 20X0	2,000	3,000	3,140	8,140
Premium on issue of shares during year	2,000			2,000
Retained profit of the year			582	582
Surplus on revaluation (W3)		1,500		1,500
As at 30 June 20X1	4,000	4,500	3,722	12,222

Workings

(W1) Cost of sales

		£000	£000
Opening stock			1,390
Purchases			8,280
			9,670
Less:	Closing stock		
	At cost	1,560	
Less:	Adjustment 1 (i) (90,000 – 20,000 – 80,000)	(10)	
Add:	Adjustment 1 (ii)	16	
			1,566
			8,104
Depreciation (W2)			2,176
			10,280

(W2) Depreciation

	£000
Buildings (£8,000 × 2%)	160
Plant and equipment (£12,800 × 20%)	2,560
	2,720
Cost of sales (80% × £2,720)	2,176
Distribution costs (10% × £2,720)	272
Administrative expenses (10% × £2,720)	272
	2,720

Answer 44

Lark (ACCA 6/00)

> ***Tutorial note:***
>
> You must be able to reproduce the FRS 3 format for the profit and loss account.
>
> **Not required** - A balance sheet.

LARK LIMITED
PROFIT AND LOSS ACCOUNT FOR THE YEAR ENDED 31 MARCH 20X0

	Continuing operations	*Discontinued operations*	*Total*
	£000	*£000*	*£000*
Sales	14,000	6,000	20,000
Cost of sales	(7,500)	(4,800)	(12,300)
Gross profit	6,500	1,200	7,700
Distribution costs	(1,260)	(840)	(2,100)
Administrative expenses	(2,290)	(700)	(2,990)
Operating profit/(loss)	2,950	(340)	2,610
Cost of fundamental reorganisation	(210)		(210)
Loss on sale of discontinued division		(400)	(400)
Profit/loss on ordinary activities before interest	2,740	(740)	2,000
Interest receivable			1,200
Interest payable			(800)
Profit on ordinary activities before taxation			2,400
Taxation			(480)
Profit for the financial year			1,920

Note. The operating profit on continuing operations of £2,950,000 is after charging an exceptionally large bad debt of £360,000 incurred during the year.

Answer 45

Notes or statements

Additional statements or notes

(i) **Statement of total recognised gains and losses**

This statement brings together the recognised gains (both realised and unrealised) which have arisen during the period from whatever source.

This statement contains:

- Profit for the financial year.
- Unrealised surplus or loss on revaluation of assets.
- Prior year adjustments.

(ii) **Reconciliation of movements in shareholders' funds**

This reconciliation sets out the effect on shareholders' funds of the various changes that occurred during the period.

This statement contains:

- Opening and closing shareholders' funds.
- Profit for the financial year.
- Dividends paid and proposed for the year.
- New share capital subscribed.
- Other recognised gains and losses.

(iii) **Note of historical cost profits and losses**

This memorandum note restates the accounts on the basis of depreciation being charged according to the historical cost of assets rather than their revalued amounts.

It contains:

- Reported profit before taxation.
- Adjustment to gains on assets sold in the period to include revaluation gains of previous years.
- Adjustment to depreciation for difference between actual depreciation charge on revalued assets and what depreciation would have been if calculated on historical cost.

Answer 46

Moorfoot (ACCA 12/00)

> ***Tutorial note:***
>
> The question required the preparation of a company's profit and loss account and balance sheet.
>
> **Not required** - Notes to the financial statements.

MOORFOOT LIMITED
PROFIT AND LOSS ACCOUNT FOR THE YEAR ENDED 30 JUNE 20X1

	£000
Sales revenue (13,600 + 7)	13,607
Cost of sales (W1)	(7,988)
Gross profit	5,619
Distribution costs (W1)	(1,948)
Administrative expenses (W1)	(2,156)
Operating profit	1,515
Interest payable	(100)
Profit for the financial year	1,415
Dividends:	
Interim paid	(360)
Final proposed	(480)
Retained profit for the financial year	575

Workings

(W1) *Cost of sales, distribution and administrative expenses*

	Cost of sales £000	*Distribution costs £000*	*Administrative expenses £000*
Purchases (8,100 + 18)	8,118		
Stock 1 July 20X0	1,530		
Distribution costs (1,460 + 120 - 60)		1,520	
Administrative expenses (1,590 + 190 – 70)			1,710
Bad debts			6
Increase in provision for doubtful debts			12
Depreciation:			
Buildings 2% × 8,300		83	83
Equipment 15% × 1,800		135	135
Vehicles 25% × 1,680		210	210
Stock 30 June 20X1	(1,660)		
	7,988	1,948	2,156

Answer 47

GAAP and FRS 3

(a) (i) Share premium is part of the capital of the company and not part of the distributable reserves (no profit is made upon issue of shares at a premium).

(ii) A revaluation reserve is an unrealised profit (ie it does not get recorded in the profit and loss account). Only realised profits should be distributed.

(b) Quality of information is improved by FRS 3.

(i) Divisional performance is highlighted by the split between continuing and discontinued activities.

(ii) Exceptional items are separately identified, which is vital when performing year on year comparatives of company performance. Figures were previously distorted by inclusion of all exceptional items as general expense headings.

(iii) All recognised gains and losses are accounted for and identified, not just the amounts included in the profit and loss account.

Answer 48

Prince plc

Consolidated balance sheet at 31 December 20X4

	£	£
Fixed assets		
Intangible assets: Goodwill (W3)		4,000
Tangible assets		140,000
		144,000
Current assets	176,000	
Creditors: Amounts falling due within one year	(91,000)	
Net current assets		85,000
Total assets less current liabilities		229,000
Creditors: Amounts falling due after more than one year		(48,000)
		181,000
Capital and reserves		
Called up share capital		60,000
Profit and loss account (W4)		121,000
		181,000

Workings

(1) Group structure

Prince
| 100%
Madonna

(2) Net assets at acquisition

	Madonna
	£
Share capital	50,000
Profit and loss account	4,000
	54,000

(3) Goodwill schedule

	Madonna
	£
Cost of investment	60,000
Net assets acquired	(54,000)
Goodwill	6,000
Less: amortisation (⅓)	(2,000)
	4,000

(4) Profit and loss account schedule

	£
P	122,000
M's post-acquisition profit	1,000
	123,000
Less: Goodwill amortisation (W3)	(2,000)
	121,000

Answer 49

Heavy plc

Consolidated balance sheet as on 31 March 20X1

	£	£
Fixed assets:		
Intangible assets: Goodwill (W3)		2,240
Tangible assets (180 + 40)		220,000
		222,240
Current assets		
Stocks (40 + 32)	72,000	
Cash at bank and in hand	13,500	
	85,500	
Creditors: Amounts falling due within one year		
Bank loans and overdrafts	14,000	
Trade creditors (41 + 17)	58,000	
Proposed dividends – parent company	10,000	
	82,000	
Net current assets		3,500
Total assets less current liabilities		225,740
Creditors: Amounts falling due after more than one year		
Debenture loans		(50,000)
		175,740
Capital and reserves		
Called-up share capital – £1 ordinary shares		100,000
Share premium account		20,000
Profit and loss account (W5)		42,040
		162,040
Minority interests (W4)		13,700
		175,740

Workings

(W1) Group structure

H

| 80%

S

(W2) Net assets of Side Ltd

	Date of acquisition	*Balance sheet date*
	£	£
Share capital	10,000	10,000
Share premium	10,000	10,000
Profit and loss	38,000	48,500
	58,000	68,500

Reserves at acquisition = £48,500 – £10,500 = £38,000

(W3) Goodwill

	£
Cost of acquisition	49,200
Share of net assets acquired 80% × 58,000 (W2)	(46,400)
	2,800
Less: amortisation ($\frac{1}{5}$)	(560)
	2,240

(W4) Minority interest

20% × 68,500 (W2)	13,700

(W5) Profit and loss

	£
Heavy plc	44,200
Dividend proposed	(10,000)
Side Ltd post-acquisition [80% × (48,500 – 38,000) (W2)]	8,400
Goodwill (W3)	(560)
	42,040

Answer 50

Roxy

> ***Tutorial note:***
>
> The information given in this question is typical of a question on cash flow statements. You should start by setting up proformas for the actual cash flow statement, starting with the net cash flow from operating activities and the reconciliation of operating profit to net cash flow.

CASH FLOW STATEMENT FOR THE YEAR ENDED 30 JUNE 20X8

	£	£
Net cash inflow from operating activities (Note)		4,050
Interest paid (W5)		(500)
Taxation (W4)		(1,200)
Capital expenditure		
Purchase of buildings	(10,000)	
Purchase of plant and machinery (W1)	(1,000)	
Sale of plant and machinery (W3)	350	
		(10,650)
Financing		
Part repayment of loan		(4,000)
Decrease in cash (11,000 + 1,300)		(12,300)

Note to the cash flow statement

Reconciliation of operating profit to net cash inflow from operating activities

	£
Operating profit	15,400
Depreciation (3,000 + 1,000 (W2))	4,000
Profit on sale of fixed assets (W3)	(100)
Increase in stock	(5,000)
Increase in debtors	(7,250)
Decrease in creditors	(3,000)
	4,050

Workings

(W1) *Plant and machinery - Cost*

	£		£
Brought forward	5,000	Disposal	1,000
Additions (balancing figure)	1,000	Carried forward	5,000
	6,000		6,000

(W2) *Plant and machinery – Accumulated depreciation*

	£		£
Disposal	750	Brought forward	2,000
Carried forward	2,250	Depreciation charge for the year (balancing figure)	1,000
	3,000		3,000

(W3) *Plant and machinery (Disposals)*

	£		£
Cost	1,000	Accumulated depreciation	750
Profit on sale	100	Proceeds	350
	1,100		1,100

(W4) *Tax creditor*

	£		£
Cash paid (balancing figure)	1,200	Brought forward	1,000
Carried forward	1,800	Profit and loss tax charge	2,000
	3,000		3,000

(W5) *Interest creditor*

	£		£
Cash paid (balancing figure)	500	Brought forward	200
Carried forward	700	Profit and loss charge	1,000
	1,200		1,200

Answer 51

Rapier (ACCA 12/97)

> ***Tutorial note:***
>
> This question concerned cash flow statements using the indirect method in FRS 1 format (ie calculating the net cash inflow from operating activities by starting with the operating profit).
>
> **Not required** - The note reconciling net cash flow with movement in net debt.

(a) *CASH FLOW STATEMENT FOR THE YEAR ENDED 30 SEPTEMBER 20X7*

	£000	*£000*
Net cash inflow from operating activities (Note 1)		161
Returns on investments and servicing of finance		
Interest paid (10% × 100,000)		(10)
Capital expenditure		
Cash to acquire fixed assets (W4)	(180)	
Cash from sale of fixed assets	25	
		(155)
Equity dividends paid		
20X6 final	18	
20X7 interim (5p × 200,000)	10	
		(28)
		(32)
Financing		
Repayment of debentures	(50)	
Proceeds of issue of shares (W5)	80	
		30
Decrease in cash (3 – 5)		(2)

Note 1 Reconciliation of operating profit to net cash inflow from operating activities

	£000
Operating profit (W1)	69
Depreciation (W2)	100
Profit on sale of fixed assets (W3)	(5)
Increase in stocks	(9)
Decrease in debtors	4
Increase in creditors	2
Net cash inflow from operating activities	161

Workings

(W1) *Operating profit*

	£000
Retained profit (203 – 176)	27
Interim dividend	10
Proposed dividend	22
Interest paid	10
Operating profit	69

(W2) *Fixed assets – aggregate depreciation*

	£000		£000
Disposal (100 – 20)	80	Brought forward	220
Carried forward	240	*Balance – profit and loss*	100
	320		320

(W3) *Fixed assets - disposal*

	£000		£000
Cost	100	Depreciation (100 – 20)	80
Balance profit and loss	5	Proceeds	25
	105		105

(W4) *Fixed assets - cost*

	£000		£000
Brought forward	600	Disposals	100
Revaluation	50	Carried forward	730
Additions – balancing figure	180		
	830		830

(W5) *Share issue*

	£000
Share capital (200 – 150)	50
Share premium (80 – 50)	30
	80

Answer 52

Weasel (ACCA 12/99)

> ***Tutorial note:***
>
> This question required a cash flow statement prepared using the indirect method under FRS 1 format. This is a standard question in the examination and you must be able to produce a proforma for this statement.
>
> **Not required** - Notes other than the reconciliation of operating profit to operating cash flows.

WEASEL PLC CASH FLOW STATEMENT YEAR ENDED 31 AUGUST 20X1

	£000	*£000*
Cash flow from operating activities (see below)		2,660
Returns on investments and servicing of finance		
Interest paid		(150)
Taxation		(400)
Capital expenditure		
Purchase of tangible fixed assets	(2,500)	
Proceeds of sale of tangible fixed assets	250	
		(2,250)
Equity dividends paid		(500)
Cash outflow before financing		(640)
Financing		
Issue of ordinary share capital	400	
Issue of debentures	500	
		900
Increase in cash in the period (300 – 200 + 360 – 200)		260

Reconciliation of operating profit to operating cash flow

Operating profit (W1)	1,710
Depreciation	1,200
Profit on sale of plant (W2)	(50)
Increase in stock	(200)
Decrease in debtors	100
Decrease in creditors	(100)
Net cash flow from operating activities	2,660

Workings

(W1) *Profit and loss account*

	£000		£000
Interest paid	150	Opening balance b/f	2,400
Taxation	500	Operating profit	1,710
Dividend paid	500		
Closing balance c/f	2,960		
	4,110		4,110

(W2) *Profit on sale of plant*

	£000
Net book value of plant disposed of per Note 1 (1,000 – 800)	200
Proceeds of sale, Note 4	250
Profit on sale	50

Answer 53

Fintry (ACCA 12/00)

> ***Tutorial note:***
>
> This is a typical question for cash flow statements and you must be able to produce the format for this statement and reconciliation.

FINTRY LIMITED
CASH FLOW STATEMENT YEAR ENDED 30 SEPTEMBER 20X1

Reconciliation of operating profit to net cash flow from operating activities

	£000
Operating profit (W2)	628
Depreciation (W1)	460
Profit on sale of fixed assets (W1)	(15)
Increase in stocks	(110)
Decrease in debtors	30
Increase in creditors	50
Net cash inflow from operating activities	1,043

Cash flow statement

	£000	£000
Net cash inflow from operating activities		1,043
Returns on investments and servicing of finance		
Interest paid (120 + 8)		(128)
Capital expenditure		
Payments to acquire fixed assets (W1)	(2,055)	
Proceeds of sale of fixed assets (W1)	55	
		(2,000)
		(1,085)
Equity dividends paid (W3)		(100)
Financing		
Issue of ordinary shares	700	
Issue of debentures	500	
		1,200
Increase in cash (W4)		15

Workings

(W1) *Fixed assets*

Fixed assets – cost or valuation

	£000		£000
Opening balance b/f	2,740	Disposal account	200
Revaluation reserve	400		
Cash – additions	2,055	Closing balance c/f	4,995
	5,195		5,195

Fixed assets – accumulated depreciation

	£000		£000
Disposal account	160	Opening balance b/f	700
Closing balance c/f	1,000	Profit and loss account – depreciation	460
	1,160		1,160

Fixed assets - disposal

	£000		£000
Fixed assets – cost	200	Fixed assets – depreciation	160
Profit and loss account - profit on sale	15	Cash proceeds	55
	215		215

(W2) *Operating profit*

Profit and loss account

	£000		£000
Dividends		Opening balance b/f	400
Interim paid	40	Operating profit	628
Final proposed	80		
Interest on debentures	120		
Interest on bank overdraft	8		
Closing balance c/f	780		
	1,028		1,028

(W3) *Dividends paid*

Dividends

	£000		£000
Cash - 20X0 final dividend	60	Opening balance b/f	60
- 20X1 interim dividend	40	Profit and loss account	
		Interim 20X1	40
Closing balance c/f	80	Final 20X1	80
	180		180

(W4) *Movement in cash*

	£000	£000
Balance at 1 October 20X0		
Cash at bank	10	
Overdraft	(80)	
		(70)
Balance at 30 September 20X1		
Cash at bank	15	
Overdraft	(70)	
		(55)
Net increase in cash		15

Answer 54

Emerald (ACCA 6/97)

> ***Tutorial note:***
>
> You must be prepared to comment on the significance of ratios as well as doing the calculations.

(a)

		Emerald Limited		*Garnet Limited*	
(i)	Current ratio	680/380	= 1.79 : 1	510/520	= 0.98 : 1
(ii)	Quick ratio	470/380	= 1.24 : 1	340/520	= 0.65 : 1
(iii)	Return on capital employed	235/1,185 × 100	= 19.8%	87/438 × 100	= 19.9%
(iv)	Return on owners' equity	225/1,085 × 100	= 20.7%	57/138 × 100	= 41.3%
(v)	Gross profit margin	360/1,075 × 100	= 33.5%	182/756 × 100	= 24.1%
(vi)	Net profit margin	235/1,075 × 100	= 21.9%	87/756 × 100	= 11.5%

(b) *Profitability*

Both Emerald and Garnet are reporting profits, though Emerald's is considerably greater.

Return on capital employed is virtually the same for both companies but return on owners' equity for Garnet is almost double that of Emerald, reflecting the high gearing due to the 10% debentures.

Garnet is borrowing at 10% but generating a return of 19.9%.

Emerald shows higher gross profit and net profit percentages, but Garnet's results are not unacceptable.

Liquidity

Emerald has an overdraft but from both the current and quick ratio shows no problems with liquidity for a manufacturing company.

Garnet has almost three times the overdraft and no bank balance, which is reflected in the ratio results giving a not too favourable picture.

However, the overdraft is often considered to be a medium or long-term method of financing, even though it is in effect a current liability, being repayable on demand.

If the overdraft was excluded on the basis of it being used on longer-term financing, it turns the liquidity into a much more favourable picture (current ratio 2.13 : 1, quick ratio 1.42 : 1).

Answer 55

Beta (ACCA 12/98)

> ***Tutorial note:***
>
> This question required the calculation of accounting ratios and interpretation of their meaning, followed by an explanation of the implications of different levels of gearing. When choosing your ratios, ensure you cover both liquidity and working capital management.

(a) Choose 4 ratios from the following:

	Zeta Ltd	*Omega Ltd*
Liquidity		
Current ratio	$\frac{1{,}350}{1{,}200}$	$\frac{1{,}880}{990}$
	= 1.13 : 1	= 1.90 : 1
Quick ratio	$\frac{950}{1{,}200}$	$\frac{1{,}080}{990}$
	= 0.79 : 1	= 1.09 : 1
Working capital management		
Stock turnover	$\frac{400}{3{,}000} \times 365$	$\frac{800}{4{,}800} \times 365$
	= 49 days	= 61 days
Debtor days	$\frac{800}{4{,}000} \times 365$	$\frac{900}{6{,}000} \times 365$
	= 73 days	= 55 days
Creditor days	$\frac{800}{3{,}200} \times 365$	$\frac{800}{4{,}800} \times 365$
	= 91 days	= 61 days

(b)

> ***Tutorial note:***
>
> The important point here is not just interpretation but comparison of the two companies as well.

(i) *Liquidity*

Here Omega shows the better position partly because Zeta has an overdraft and no cash balance.

However, Omega has a much higher stock figure. Depending on the reason, this could actually distort the current ratio to give a rosier picture.

(ii) *Working capital management*

Omega has better credit control for its debtors but is not as successful at turning over stock. Omega may also consider lengthening creditors' payment period to be consistent with the industry average.

Zeta has a more efficient stock turnover rate but its debtor and creditor management reinforces its liquidity problem.

Both companies are at least paying their creditors after collecting cash from debtors.

(c) High gearing suggests a high financial risk.

Consider whether the return of each company is greater than the rate of interest of any financing, Zeta has no significant financing and therefore no gearing.

However, Omega has 10% debentures which creates gearing. Omega's return on capital employed is 11.6% which is just above financing rate.

From a risk point of view, Zeta would survive a fall in trade, whereas if Omega's return were to fall as a result and drop below 10%, it could have an adverse effect for shareholders.

An increase in trade would have more of an impact for Omega by increasing the margin between the financing interest rate and Omega's return.

Answer 56

Hawk (ACCA 12/00)

> ***Tutorial note:***
>
> This question requires eight accounting ratios. Choose ratios that cover the obvious areas of profitability, liquidity and working capital management.
>
> **Not required** - Definitions of the ratios.

(a)

	Year ended 31 March *20X0*	*20X1*
Profitability		
(i) Gross profit percentage –		
Gross profit as percentage of sales		
$600/1{,}800 \times 100\%$	33.3%	
$700/2{,}500 \times 100\%$		28.0%
(ii) Net profit as a percentage of sales –		
Operating profit as a percentage of sales revenue		
$240/1{,}800 \times 100\%$	13.3%	
$250/2{,}500 \times 100\%$		10.0%

(iii)	Return on owners' equity		
	190/1,568 × 100%	12.1%	
	200/2,122 × 100%		9.4%
(iv)	Return on capital employed (ROCE)		
	240/2,068 × 100%	11.6%	
	250/2,622 × 100%		9.5%
Liquidity			
(iv)	Current ratio		
	700 : 518	1.35 : 1	
	1,230 : 860		1.43 : 1
(v)	Quick ratio		
	500 : 518	0.96 : 1	
	870 : 860		1.01 : 1

(Note the question requirement to use closing figures for the balance sheet items needed.)

(b) *Comments on ratios*

(i) Gross profit percentage on sales has declined from 33.3% to 28.0%, a drop of 16%. This is possibly due to a decision to lower prices to increase sales revenue, which has risen by 38.9%. A drop in the gross profit percentage is an indicator of possible error or fraud if an explanation such as a lowering of prices cannot be found.

(ii) Net profit as a percentage of sales is down from 13.3% to 10%, down about 25%. The net profit percentage has fallen more than the gross profit percentage, probably because distribution costs have risen sharply.

(iii) Return on capital employed has declined from 11.6% to 9.5%, a drop of about 18%. This is a reflection of the decline in profitability shown by ratio (ii) above).

(iv) and (v)
The two ratios measuring liquidity have changed little between the two periods and are satisfactory at both dates.

Answer 57

Goodwill

> ***Tutorial note:***
>
> This question tested standard bookwork on goodwill and should have provided easy marks.

Goodwill is defined as 'the difference between the value of a business as a whole and the aggregate of the fair values of its separable net assets'.

(a) A business will create goodwill mainly from its relationship with its customers. This could be based on the following.

- Attitude and experience of its staff
- Reputation, reliability and quality of its products or services
- Location of the business

(b) Inherent or non-purchased goodwill is the goodwill generated within the business as it grows, for the reasons discussed above. It is very difficult to value as it has no cash value attached to it. It is also open to large fluctuations based on changes in the factors above.

Purchased goodwill is inherent goodwill which has had a value attached to it by being bought together with the business on which it has grown.

When a business is sold, if the purchaser and seller agree on a price for the business which is greater than the value of the net assets, then purchased goodwill arises.

(c) *Accounting treatment*

Inherent goodwill should never be included in the balance sheet. Although it may be accepted that it exists, it should never be included as an asset.

The main reason for not including inherent goodwill in the balance sheet is the uncertainty of its value.

Purchased goodwill has had a value attached to it when the business has changed ownership. It is therefore included in the balance sheet as an intangible asset.

In line with other fixed assets, goodwill is then amortised through the profit and loss account over the useful economic life of the goodwill on a straight line basis.

In accordance with FRS 10 there is a rebuttable presumption that the useful economic life is a maximum of 20 years.

However, where it can be demonstrated that goodwill is durable and is capable of continued measurement, it may be amortised over a life greater than 20 years.

Where goodwill is regarded as having an indefinite life, it is carried as a permanent intangible asset and no amortisation is charged.

The useful economic life should be reviewed at the end of each accounting period.

Any negative goodwill is carried as a negative intangible asset under any positive goodwill.

Impairment reviews should be carried out to highlight a fall in value, as follows.

- At the end of the accounting period following acquisition.
- Where a useful economic life of less than 20 years is used (when an indication of a fall in value has occurred).
- Where a useful economic life of more than 20 years is used, a review is carried out every year.

Answer 58

Standards (ACCA 6/97)

> ***Tutorial note:***
>
> Each of the points relates to a different accounting standard (SSAP 17 and FRS 12); compare the treatment in the company's financial statements with the requirements of the standard and decide whether this is acceptable.
>
> **Not required** - General discussion of these standards.

(a) *Post balance sheet events (SSAP 17)*

Under SSAP 17 a post balance sheet event is an event which occurs between the balance sheet date and the date on which the financial statements are approved by the board of directors.

The debtor existed at the balance sheet date and the liquidation of the major debtor provides more information about that debtor.

In accordance with SSAP 17, this is an adjusting event which would require the bad debt to be written off in this year's financial statements, as has been done.

(b) *Contingency*

FRS 12 gives guidance on the accounting treatment for contingent assets and liabilities which do not meet the recognition requirements for an asset or liability.

A contingent loss should be accrued if it is probable that a future event will confirm that loss. It must be able to be estimated with reasonable certainty.

However, a contingent liability need only be disclosed in a note to the financial statements (rather than being accrued for). If its occurrence is very unlikely it can be ignored.

In this case, as the claim is unlikely to succeed, FRS 12 would require the damages estimate to be disclosed in a note. Also, as the legal costs will be incurred regardless, a provision should be made in the financial statements.

Answer 59

Rubens (ACCA 12/98)

> ***Tutorial note:***
>
> This question was about the provisions of SSAP 13 Research and Development.
>
> **Not required** - Discussion of SSAP 13 or its criteria for development expenditure.

(a) Criteria for capitalising development expenditure

- A defined project exists.
- The expenditure is separately identifiable.
- The project is technically feasible.
- The project is commercially viable.
- The future profits will exceed the total expenditure incurred.
- Sufficient resources are available to complete the project.

(b) *Profit and loss extract*

	£000
Research and development (W1)	3,940

To be included in cost of sales.

Balance sheet extract

	£000
Deferred development expenditure (W3)	7,560

To be included as a separate heading in intangible fixed assets.

Workings

(W1)

	£000	£000
Current year expenditure		
Research		1,800
Project D costs		300
		2,100
Previous year's expenditure written off		1,200
Amortisation of deferred expenditure (W2)		640
		3,940

(W2) *Amortisation*

	£000
Project A 20X5 – 20X7 $\frac{1}{5} \times 1{,}000{,}000$	200
Project B November 20X7 – September 20X8 $(\frac{1}{5} \times 2{,}400) \times \frac{11}{12}$	440
	640

(W3) *Movements in deferred expenditure*

Project	*Bfwd* £000	*Expenditure* £000	*Written off* £000	*Amortisation* £000	*Capital* £000	*Cfwd* £000
A	600			200		400
B	2,400			440		1,960
C	3,600				400	4,000
D	1,200	300	1,500			
E					800	800
F					400	400
	7,800	300	1,500	640	1,600	7,560

Answer 60

Ochil (ACCA 12/00)

> *Tutorial note:*
>
> This question covered SSAP 17 and relevant parts of FRS 12.
>
> **Not required** - General discussion of the standards.

(a) Post balance sheet events fall into two categories:

(i) Adjusting events which provide additional evidence of conditions existing at the balance sheet date.

(ii) Non-adjusting events which concern conditions which did not exist. However, additional disclosure is required if the events are material – by way of a note to the financial statements.

There are four categories of contingencies – depending on whether the likelihood is remote, possible, probable or virtually certain (in which case the item would not fall within the definition of a contingency).

Likelihood of occurrence	*Treatment of material contingent liability*
Remote	No disclosure
Possible	Disclose by note
Probable	Set up provision

(b) Events in the financial statements:

(1) This is an adjusting post balance sheet event under SSAP 17. The stock should be reduced by £40,000 (£200,000 - £160,000) in the trading account and balance sheet (SSAP 17).

(2) This is another adjusting post balance sheet event under SSAP 17. The provision for doubtful debts should be reduced by £65,000 and profit and loss account credited (SSAP 17).

(3) The £50,000 claim for damages is a contingency which requires disclosure by note only as it is not probable that a liability will arise. Provision should be made in the March 20X1 accounts for the £10,000 legal costs (FRS 12).

(4) Provision should be made for the £100,000 probable liability under the guarantee (FRS 12).

(5) The proposed merger is a non-adjusting post balance sheet event and should be disclosed by note in the financial statements for the year ended 31 March 20X1 (SSAP 17).

(6) This is an adjusting balance sheet event under SSAP 17 and the stock figure should be increased by £30,000 cost.

(c) Effect on profit:

		£	£
Profit as shown in draft accounts			350,000
Add:	Reduction in doubtful debt provision (2)	65,000	
	Stock omitted (6)	30,000	
			95,000
			445,000
Less:	Reduction in value of stock (1)	40,000	
	Provision for legal costs (3)	10,000	
	Provision for guarantee liability (4)	100,000	
			150,000
Revised profit			295,000

Answer 61

SSAP 13 (ACCA 12/00)

> ***Tutorial note:***
> This question related to development expenditure under SSAP 13.
> **Not required** - General discussion of SSAP 13.

(a) The conditions which must be met if development expenditure is to be capitalised are:

(i) There is a clearly defined project.

(ii) The related expenditure is separately identifiable.

(iii) The outcome of the project has been assessed with reasonable certainty as to:

- Technical feasibility
- Commercial viability

(iv) Future sales revenues will exceed the aggregate of development costs to date plus future development costs, together with production, selling and administration costs.

(v) Adequate resources exist to enable the project to be completed and to provide any consequential increases in working capital.

Answer 62

Lomond (ACCA 12/00)

(a) *For the year ended 30 June 20X3*

	Profit and loss account £	*Balance sheet* £
Project A		
Amortisation (£200,000 ÷ 5)	40,000	
Balance sheet (£200,000 – (3 × £40,000))		80,000
Project B		
Expenditure written off (£175,000 + £55,000)	230,000	Nil
Project C		
Development expenditure to date (£85,000 + £170,000)		255,000
Project D		
Research expenditure	80,000	Nil
	350,000	335,000

(b) The notes required by SSAP 13 are:

(i) Total research and development expenditure charged in the profit and loss account was £350,000 comprising:

	£
Expenditure during the year £(55,000 + 80,000)	135,000
Amortised or written off from deferred expenditure £(40,000 + 175,000)	215,000
	£350,000

(ii) Movements on deferred development expenditure:

	£
Balance at 1 July 20X2 £(120,000 + 175,000 + 85,000)	380,000
Expenditure in current year £(55,000 + 170,000)	225,000
	605,000
Amortised during year	(40,000)
Expenditure on abandoned project written off (from (b))	(230,000)
Balance at 30 June 20X3	£335,000

ANSWERS TO PILOT PAPER

These answers have been produced by The Financial Training Company

PILOT PAPER ANSWERS

Section A

Answer 63 (Answer 1 of Pilot Paper)

(i) A correct;

B Sales would be a debit;

C Interest charged would be a debit;

D As B & C.

(ii) B

	£
Correction of repairs profit understated	38,000
Depreciation charge profit overstated (20% × 38,000) × $\frac{3}{12}$	1,900
Total understated	36,100

(iii) D

Suspense account

	£		£
Discount received	5,100	(836,200 – 819,700)	16,500
Debtors	9,900	Discount allowed	3,900
Balance b/f	5,400		
	20,400		20,400
		Balance b/f	5,400

(iv) B

1 &3 are one sided adjustments.

2 is a transfer between debtor accounts.

4 is a transfer from discount received to discount allowed.

5 a complete journal is required.

(v) B $\frac{5}{12} \times \left(\frac{30{,}000 - 6{,}000}{4}\right)$

(vi) C

A & D carriage outwards not allowed.

B cost of storage not allowed.

(vii) C

	Cost	*NRV*
400 items	400 × £4	(400 × £3) - 200
	£1,600	£1,000
Use £1,000		
200 items	200 × £30	(200 × £35) – 1,200 – 300
	£6,000	£5,500
Use £5,500		

Total stock value = 116,400 + 1,000 + 5,500 = £122,900

(viii) D

(ix) C

	£
Bank statement balance	(38,600)
Add uncredited deposits	41,200
Less outstanding cheques	(3,300)
	(700)

(x) A

3 & 4 are bank reconciliation statement items.

(xi) A

Debtors

	£		£
Bfwd	29,100	Cash	381,600
		Cash	6,800
Refunds	2,100	Bad debts	7,200
Sales	412,400	Discount allowed	9,400
		Cfwd	38,600
	443,600		443,600

	£
Credit sales	412,400
Cash sales	112,900
	525,300

(xii) D

Cost structure		£	£
100%	Sales (bal.)		140,000
	Opening stock	17,000	
	Purchases	91,000	
		108,000	
	Closing stock	(24,000)	
60%	Cost of sales		84,000
40%	Gross profit		56,000

Gross profit 84,000 × $^{40}/_{60}$ = 56,000

(xiii) A

Rent

	£		£
Bfwd ⅔ × 6,000	4,000	P & L	27,500
1.4 cash	6,000		
1.7 cash	7,500		
1.10 cash	7,500		
1.1 cash	7,500	Cfwd ⅔ × 7,500	5,000
	32,500		32,500

24,000 ÷ 4 = £6,000 per quarter.

30,000 ÷ 4 = £7,500 per quarter.

(xiv) B

	£
Stock @ cost 1.12.2000	28,400
Purchased @ cost	49,600
	78,000
Sales 64,800 × $^{70}/_{100}$	(45,360)
Closing stock destroyed	32,640

(xv) D

1 All research costs are written off immediately.

4 Amortisation commences at commercial production.

(xvi) A

	D	*E*	*F*
	£	£	£
Old agreement	5	3	2
Profit ($\frac{6}{12} \times 480{,}000$)	108,000	64,800	43,200
Salaries ($\frac{6}{12} \times 24{,}000$)		12,000	12,000
	108,000	76,800	55,200
New agreement	3	1	1
Profit share ($\frac{6}{12} \times 480{,}000$)	126,000	42,000	42,000
Salaries		18,000	12,000
	126,000	60,000	54,000
Total	234,000	136,800	109,200

(xvii) C

	Share capital	*Share premium*
	£	£
Opening balance	500,000	300,000
Share issue (200,000 × 50p)	100,000	
Premium (200,000 × 80p)		160,000
	600,000	
Bonus issue (£600,000 ÷ 50p) × $\frac{1}{4}$ = 300,000 shares		
(300,000 × 50p)		
= £150,000	150,000	(150,000)
	750,000	310,000

(xviii) B

Division is discontinuing for 2000 but the gain is not realised until 2001.

(xix) B

A	Interest paid is a cash item.
C	Equity dividends paid are a cash item.
D	As A & C.

(xx) B

A	Adjust for the debtor.
C	Discovery of fraud or error.
D	Sale of stock giving evidence is adjusted.

(xxi) D

A	Lack of chasing debtors.
B	Proportionate debtors and sales.
C	Won't impact collection time.

(xxii) B

(xxiii) B

H

80%

S

Net assets	*At acq.*
	£
Share capital	100,000
Reserves	40,000
	140,000

	£
Purchase consideration	160,000
For 80% net assets at acq. (80% × 140,000)	(112,000)
Goodwill	48,000

Amortisation to date ($\frac{3}{5}$ × 40,000)	(28,800)
Goodwill remaining	19,200

(xxiv) D

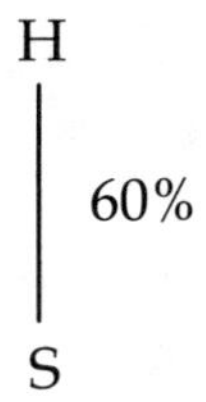

Net assets	*At BS Date*
	£
Share capital	100,000
Reserves	180,000
	280,000

Minority interest

	£
40% net assets at BS date (40% × 280,000)	112,000

(xxv) C

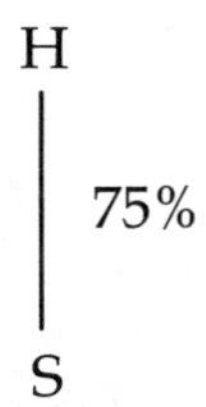

Net assets	*At date acq.*
	£
Share capital	200,000
P & L reserves	120,000
	320,000

	£
Purchase consideration	280,000
For 75% net assets at acq. (75% × 320,000)	(240,000)
Goodwill	40,000

P & L reserve

	£
100% H	480,000
75% S post acq. reserves	

180,000 31.12.00 → pre acq. 120,000 1.1.94

180,000 31.12.00 → post acq. 60,000

	£
75% × 60,000	45,000
Less goodwill fully amortised	(40,000)
	485,000

Section B

Answer 64 (Answer 2 of Pilot Paper)

Materiality

The omission or mis-statement of an item in a financial statement is material if, in the light of surrounding circumstances, the magnitude of the item is such that it is probable that the judgement of a reasonable person relying upon the report would have been changed or influenced by the inclusion or correction of the item.

There is no rigid or officially recognised definition. It is a practical rule.

It allows other rules to be ignored if the consequences of doing so are considered insignificant and out of all proportion to the time and cost involved in rigidly following those other rules.

For example: a stock loss would be disclosed if it were material.

Substance over form

Under this concept, transactions and other events are accounted for and presented in financial statements in accordance with their economic substance and financial reality and not merely with their legal form.

For example, leasehold buildings are owned by the landlord rather than the occupier. But the occupier is using them for his business in the same way as if they were freehold. Thus it is appropriate to treat them as a fixed asset, provided that it is made clear that the premises are leasehold.

For example: an asset 'acquired' under a finance lease is treated as an asset even though legal title isn't transferred.

Money measurement

Only items which have a monetary value attributed to them will be recorded in the accounts.

Although all items have a value the problem comes in defining the monetary value. Valuation of less tangible items may be impossible.

For example: inherent goodwill cannot reasonably be assessed in value and therefore should not be included in the balance sheet.

Answer 65 (Answer 3 of Pilot Paper)

(a)

		30.4.00	*30.4.01*
(i)	ROCE		
	$\frac{\text{Profit before int. \& tax}}{\text{Capital employed}}$	$\frac{5,000}{48,600}$	$\frac{6,500}{72,300}$
		= 10.3%	= 9.0%
(ii)	ROOE		
	$\frac{\text{Net profit}}{\text{Shareholders' funds}}$	$\frac{3,600}{28,600}$	$\frac{3,700}{32,300}$
		= 12.6%	= 11.5%
(iii)	Current ratio		
	$\frac{\text{Current assets}}{\text{Current liabilities}}$	$\frac{38,600}{28,500}$	$\frac{43,000}{17,400}$
		= 1.35 : 1	= 2.47 :1
(iv)	Quick ratio		
	$\frac{\text{Current assets} - \text{stock}}{\text{Current liabilities}}$	$\frac{22,200}{28,500}$	$\frac{24,600}{17,400}$
		= 0.78 : 1	= 1.41 :1
(v)	Gearing	$\frac{20,000}{48,600}$	$\frac{40,000}{72,300}$
		= 41.1%	= 55.3%

(b) ROCE and ROOE

Both have shown a fall in the period. Looking at the return, the gross profit is reasonably consistent though the operating expenses have not increased in line with increased sales.

The likely cause is that the capital raised by the debenture issue has not yet produced a return.

Current and quick ratios

Both ratios would be considered rather low in 2000, mainly due to the large overdraft.

The overdraft has been reduced by nearly two thirds, probably using the funds raised by the debenture issue.

The levels of these ratios now in 2001 have taken a turn and are rather high. This is not necessarily for the best.

As the funds from the share issue are invested these ratios should return to normal.

Gearing

The percentage of debt financing within Brood was high in 2000 but has risen to a very high level in 2001 as a result of the debenture issue.

The level of risk within Brood is high and it is going to be vulnerable to changes, particularly falls, in profit. This is highlighted by the fact that interest is almost half the profit from operations.

Answer 66 (Answer 4 of Pilot Paper)

Crash Limited

Cash flow statement for the year ended 31 March 2001

	£000	*£000*
Net cash inflow from operating activities (Note)		1,995
Returns on investments and servicing of finance		
Interest paid		(150)
Capital expenditure		
Purchase of fixed assets (W1)	(2,700)	
Proceeds of sale of fixed assets	375	
		(2,325)
		(480)
Financing		
Repayment of debentures (1,500 – 750)	(750)	
Proceeds of issue of shares (W4)	1,200	
		450
Decrease in cash (165 – 135)		(30)

Note 1. Reconciliation of operating profit to net cash inflow from operating activities.

	£000
Operating profit	555
Depreciation (W1)	1,500
Profit on sale of fixed assets (W2)	(75)
Increase in stocks (1,350 – 1,215)	(135)
Decrease in debtors (1,290 – 1,350)	60
Increase in creditors (1,080 – 990)	90
Net cash inflow from operating activities	1,995

W1 **Fixed assets – cost**

	£000		£000
Bfwd	9,000	Disposals	1,500
Revaluation	750		
Cash	2,700	Cfwd	10,950
	12,450		12,450

W2 **Fixed assets – depreciation**

	£000		£000
Disposals	1,200	Bfwd	3,300
		Profit & loss account	1,500
Cfwd	3,600		
	4,800		4,800

W3 **Fixed assets – disposal**

	£000		£000
Cost	1,500	Accum. depreciation	1,200
Profit & loss account – profit	75	Proceeds of sale	375
	1,575		1,575

W4 **Share issue**

	£000
Share capital (3,000 – 2,250)	750
Share premium (1,200 – 750)	450
	1,200

Answer 67 (Answer 5 of Pilot Paper)

To: The Directors of Jurien Ltd

From: Financial Accountant

Date: June 2001

Subject: *Accounting Treatment of Items in the Financial Statements*

In response to your enquiry, I have considered the three situations, my advice is outlined below.

(a) **Food poisoning**

In accordance with FRS 12 Provisions, contingent liabilities and contingent assets where a liability is probable a provision should be recognised in the balance sheet.

To define: a liability is a probable present obligation from a past event.

This is exactly the situation here, provision must be made for a reasonable estimate of the amount needed to settle the obligation.

(b) **Trade debtor**

This falls under the guidance of SSAP 17 Post Balance Sheet Events which classifies events after the balance sheet date as adjusting or non-adjusting.

In order for a provision to be made in the financial statements the event must be adjusting.

To qualify as an adjusting event there must be evidence that the financial difficulties were being encountered by the debtor at the balance sheet date. Without this evidence no provision should be made.

(c) **Stock**

Stock valuation is governed by SSAP 9 Stocks and Long Term Contracts which states 'stock is valued at the lower of cost and net realisable value'.

Cost is expenses incurred in bringing the item of stock to its present condition and location.

These expenses or overheads are allocated under the rules of SSAP 9:

(i) Only overheads directly attributable to production may be included;

(ii) The allocation of fixed production overheads must be based on the normal level of activity in the period.

Examples of overheads which must be excluded:

(i) Selling costs, which form part of the calculation of net realisable value.

(ii) Administration overheads which do not bring stock to its present location and condition.

Answer 68 (Answer 6 of Pilot Paper)

	£000	£000
Fixed assets		
Tangibles (W1)		450
Current assets		
Stocks	180	
Debtors (146 – 12)	134	
Prepayments	8	
Cash at bank and in hand	50	
	372	
Creditors: amounts falling due within one year		
Creditors	94	
Accruals	4	
	98	
Net current assets		274
Total assets less current liabilities		724
Creditors: amounts falling due after more than one year		(100)
		624
Capital and reserves		
Called up share capital (W4)		350
Share premium account (W4)		240
Profit and loss account		34
		624

Workings

W1 Tangible fixed assets

	Land & Buildings £000	Plant & Equipment £000	Total £000
Cost			
At 1.4.2000	410	318	728
Additions	-	-	-
Disposals	-	(18)	(18)
At 31.3.2001	410	300	710
Accum. depreciation			
At 1.4.2000	120	88	208
Disposals (W2)	-	(12)	(12)
Depreciation charge (W3)	4	60	64
At 31.3.2001	124	136	260
NBV 1.4.2000	290	230	520
NBV 31.3.2001	286	164	450

W2 Depreciation on disposal

	£
Cost	18,000
NBV	(6,000)
Accum. depreciation	12,000

W3 Depreciation charge

	£
Buildings (2% × 200,000)	4,000
Plant & equipment	
Cost at 1.4.2000	318,000
Disposal	(18,000)
	300,000
Depreciation charge	
20% × 300,000	60,000

W4 Share issue

	Share Capital £	*Share Premium* £
At 1.4. 2000	250,000	180,000
Share issue 200,000 50p shares @ 30p premium	100,000	60,000
	350,000	240,000

Exam Kit Review Form

ACCA PAPER 1.1 KIT – PREPARING FINANCIAL STATEMENTS (UK)

We hope that you have found this Kit stimulating and useful and that you now feel confident and well-prepared for your examinations.

We would be grateful if you could take a few moments to complete the questionnaire below, so we can assess how well our material meets your needs. There's a prize for four lucky students who fill in one of these forms from across the Syllabus range and are lucky enough to be selected!

	Excellent	*Adequate*	*Poor*
Depth and breadth of technical coverage			
Appropriateness of coverage to examination			
Presentation			
Level of accuracy			

Did you spot any errors or ambiguities? Please let us have the details below.

Page	**Error**

Thank you for your feedback.

Please return this form to:

The Financial Training Company Limited
Unit 2, Block 2, Wincombe Conference Centre
Wincombe Business Park
Shaftesbury
Dorset SP7 9QJ

Student's name: ....

Address: ....

....

....

ACCA Publications Student Order Form

THE FINANCIAL TRAINING COMPANY
PUBLICATIONS DIVISION

To order your books, please indicate quantity required in the relevant order box, calculate the amount(s) in the column provided, and add postage to determine the amount due. Please then clearly fill in your details plus method of payment in the boxes provided and return your completed form with payment attached to:

THE FINANCIAL TRAINING COMPANY, 22J WINCOMBE BUSINESS PARK, SHAFTESBURY, DORSET SP7 9QJ
OR FAX YOUR ORDER TO 01747 858821 OR TELEPHONE 01747 854302

For examinations in Dec 03 ❑ June 04 ❑ Dec 04 ❑ (please tick)

PAPER	TITLE	TEXT ORDER	PRICE £	EXAM KIT ORDER	PRICE £	FOCUS NOTES ORDER	PRICE £	AMOUNT £
PART 1								
1.1	Preparing Financial Statements (UK)		21.00		11.00		6.00	
1.2	Financial Information for Management		21.00		11.00		6.00	
1.3	Managing People		21.00		11.00		6.00	
PART 2								
2.1	Information Systems		21.00		11.00		6.00	
2.2	Corporate and Business Law		21.00		11.00		6.00	
2.3	Business Taxation [FA2002] (June & Dec 03)		21.00		11.00		6.00	
	Business Taxation [FA2003] (June & Dec 04)		21.00	Available Jan 04	11.00	Available Jan 04	6.00	
2.4	Financial Management & Control		21.00		11.00		6.00	
2.5	Financial Reporting		21.00		11.00		6.00	
2.6	Audit & Internal Review		21.00		11.00		6.00	
PART 3								
3.1	Audit & Assurance Services		21.00		11.00		6.00	
3.2	Advanced Taxation [FA2002] (June & Dec 03)		21.00		11.00		6.00	
	Advanced Taxation [FA2003] (June & Dec 04)		21.00	Available Jan 04	11.00	Available Jan 04	6.00	
3.3	Performance Management		21.00		11.00		6.00	
3.4	Business Information Management		21.00		11.00		6.00	
3.5	Strategic Business Planning & Development		21.00		11.00		6.00	
3.6	Advanced Corporate Reporting		21.00		11.00		6.00	
3.7	Strategic Financial Management		21.00		11.00		6.00	

Sub Total	£
Postage and packing – please note a signature is required on delivery *UK & NI* £5 for up to 10 books If only Focus Notes are ordered, £1 each (max £5) **First book** / **Each additional book** *Europe* £25 / £3 *Rest of World* £40 / £4	£
TOTAL PAYMENT	£

The following section **must be filled in clearly** so that your order can be despatched without delay.

TO PAY FOR YOUR ORDER TICK AN OPTION BELOW

A. I WISH TO PAY BY MASTERCARD ❑ VISA ❑ DELTA ❑ SWITCH ❑

CARD NO. (Some cards don't need all boxes)

EXPIRY DATE ISSUE No. (Switch only) All cards - last 3 digits on signature strip

Cardholder's Signature ________________

Cardholder's Name & Address: ________________

Cardholder's Tel. No. (Day):

B. I WISH TO PAY BY CHEQUE ❑ Cheques should be made payable to *The Financial Training Company Ltd* and must be attached to your order form. **Personal cheques cannot be accepted without a valid Banker's Card number written on the back of the cheque**.

STUDENT NAME:

DELIVERY ADDRESS: (Must be the same as cardholder's address. Please contact us if you wish to discuss an alternative delivery address).

POST CODE: TEL. NO. (Day):

April 2003 (This order form replaces any previous order forms.)